INVITATION...TO ANNIHILATION

by MIKE LIPKIN

foreword by ROBB & LINDA GORDON
1987 NORTH AMERICAN IMP-PAIR CHAMPIONS

Published by
Devyn Press, Inc.
3600 Chamberlain Lane, Suite 230
Louisville, KY 40241

ISBN 0-910791-89-9

TO

the many people
who have contributed to my bridge education,
but especially to

MELVIN LAWHORN

of Chicago,
1954 ABA National Men's Pair Champion,
and a great man all years.

ACKNOWLEDGMENTS

A very large number of people helped out with this effort, my first, at book writing. Judy Cohn, Jerry Fink and Ira Herman spent enormous amounts of time reading through, commenting and correcting rough versions of this manuscript. Clay Brooke-McFarland made some valuable suggestions and Dorothee Fuchs introduced me to her daughter, Annie Campbell, the best illustrator in Ithaca, NY. Also thanks to my mother who contributed in two ways: she introduced me to bridge and she made suggestions for the illustrations.

Many of the hands used throughout the book come from actual play. Some of these were previously recorded elsewhere. In addition to the citations found in the body of the work, I should like to credit Phillip Alder, whose excellent article on Zia for the *Bridge World* provided me with three examples, Clay B.-McFarland who recalled the Oswald Jacoby hand, and Alan Truscott, whose New York Times column was the source of several others.

Finally, much thanks goes to Robert and Linda Gordon, principally for their friendship and assistance but additionally for their kind words.

FOREWORD

One subject of bridge philosophy which is often a source of debate is the relative value of different aspects of bridge skill. Some say bidding, some say declarer play or defense. In our opinion, the most important thing for an advancing player to develop is *empathy*.

Alas, this is an area until now virtually unexplored in bridge literature. Aside from chapters on "mandatory" falsecards, there is almost nothing to guide the aspiring player to this new thought process.

We have always thought that one's personal advancement in bridge comes through revelation rather than evolution. In particular, we remember when, as beginners, we first understood one of the millions (well, it *seems* like millions) of post mortems that came our way. As if somebody turned on the light and all was right there for us to see, though it had been dark moments before.

You may have read about squeezes or coups, but they didn't sink in until you actually *saw them at the table* (and maybe even executed them).

This book will take you through the process of being there. To be sure it will put you in your seat (South, as usual), but you will also magically drift to your opponents' seats, and back again. When you can bring this skill to the table with you, you will advance several rungs on the ladder of bridge success.

How fitting that Michael Lipkin, one of the nicest and most *empathic* individuals we know, should be the author of this *revolutionary* tome. We hope you enjoy it as much as we did.

Robb & Linda Gordon
New York, June 1991

Table of Contents

INVITATION TO ANNIHILATION

and Other Essays on

How to Make The Bad Guys Go Wrong

at the Bridge Table

by Mike Lipkin

Foreword by Robb and Linda Gordon,

1987 North American IMP-Pair Champions

Illustrations by Annie Campbell

INTRODUCTION
PLENTY OF PROBLEMS TO GO AROUND

All of us play badly from time to time. That much is certain. In November, 1990, at a Hartford, CT regional tournament, the audience was treated to the following startling occurrence. A national- and world-class player, leading the race for the Barry Crane national master-point award, got to $7NT$ losing a trick to the ace of clubs and made up for it by pushing to 7♠ on a subsequent hand, going down two, with six makable.

I can hear you now: "Another stupid book telling me how to cut down my errors!" WRONG. This is much more fun. This volume will introduce you to the joys of getting the other guy to go wrong. And, of course, this is not a silly notion. Remember that hand from last week. It was the zillionth board you played that night and the game was taking longer than usual. Frankly, the contract was routine, $3NT$, and they had ten top tricks. So, twelve tricks had gone by and...wait a minute...did you need to hold the ♠Q or the ◇9? D—! You didn't get it right. Afterwards, your lift home remarked innocently about the weird results that evening. "Did you see, someone made 11 tricks on that routine notrump game? You just wouldn't believe it."

However, when you went over the hand later in your mind, you realized that declarer overtook the ◇8 at trick three with dummy's K. Of course, both the ◇8 and ◇5 were each losers. It's just that routinely we eliminate the smaller cards from our hands first. Come to think of it, maybe declarer deliberately varied his routine with your impending problem in mind.

And that's the point of this book. What you will

find here are hints on how to harry your opponents, how to get them to make more of those stupid, trivial errors that the other guy's book will teach you to avoid. Frankly, many of these ideas work best against suspect opponents. You just can't count on very good players to go wrong all that often. But sometimes these techniques will be all you have to frustrate and confuse the other side. And some fraction of the time they will work, no matter how expert the bad guys are.

The origin of this work was that same Hartford regional. Watching mistakes at even the highest levels, it occurred to me that errors are not something which will ever go away. The literature has generally treated errors as aberrations (exceptions are Hugh Kelsey's writings on deceptive play), which has had the effect of excluding them from systematic regard. For books on declarer play, the defense is always perfect, or, in any case, very fine. The solution to a quiz problem is, therefore, an exact sequence of plays from which no deviation is possible, or for that matter necessary. When the topic has been defense the same was true. Both defenders solve a problem, involving communications or counting or what-have-you in a predetermined and inflexible fashion.

This book is unique in a fundamental way. Many of the contracts you will find here, illustrative of declarer play, can be defeated, or at least handled properly by the opponents. There is often no sequence of plays which will guarantee success for declarer. Similarly, each defensive problem can come to nil for the defenders. Unlike other bridge books, if you master all the techniques in this volume, on a bad day your overbidding will kill your game, and your defensive gems will come to naught. But on a good day the overtricks will be plentiful and your defenses will succeed.

Especially at match-point duplicate (pairs or Board-a-Match teams), errors have a more profound effect than perfect technique. We have all heard players bemoan the fact that they were only dealt a low match-pointing game. What they mean is that good technique would only have gotten them so far. In the currently fashionable IMP-pairs, errors are so much a part of the game that my partner and I once had a +120 IMP session in a national event, and the only decision I recall having to make was a close "bid game or not" which we got wrong. Fortunately, the opponents got around 12 decisions wrong.

There are many facets to the subject of error production, and it would be impossible to cover all the possible material. Indeed, there is still room for new ideas and ploys. Much remains to be discovered. As a result, I have chosen to omit some topics, either because they appear infrequently, or because they are discussed extensively elsewhere. One aspect of this subject which is missing from the book concerns unusual bidding systems. There is no doubt that novel and unusual conventional bids work to produce mistakes. This accounts for the initial great successes of forcing pass systems in the last decade. As a result of the forcing pass, two U.S. players declared 2♣ instead of a cold 7♡ in the world team championships. There are many other examples available. I happen to side with the minority view which finds destructive or interfering systems to be exciting and challenging contributions to the development of bridge. However, to adopt an unusual system solely for the purpose of sowing confusion is a bizarre approach to the game of bridge, unlikely to appeal to many people, and in any event not the point. We will look at techniques available to everyone as part of any partnership's normal repertoire.

Chapter 1
LENGTH BEFORE BEAUTY

You pick up ♠K108, ♡AJ4, ◇53, ♣KQ754 and open 1NT (11-14). Partner bids 2♣, Stayman, and then invites with 2NT. Since the game is IMPS and you are vulnerable, the decision isn't close; you bid 3NT and all pass. Lefty tables the ♠4 (fourth best) and this is what you get:

```
N-S VUL   ♠ Q6
DLR: S    ♡ K982
          ◇ KQ4
          ♣ J1032



          ♠ K108
          ♡ AJ4
          ◇ 53
          ♣ KQ754
```

Well, it's certainly a reasonable contract. You have 2 spades on the lead, 4 clubs and two hearts, as well as a sure diamond trick. Furthermore, the hearts will permit you additional tricks if you find the queen. Anyway, you win the first trick in hand with the ten and lead a small club to the board. RHO wins and returns a spade which lefty ducks to your queen. Time to take stock.

You have serious concerns that West began with 5 spades. His spade duck is an attempt to keep communications with partner. Since RHO should have one more spade, you can no longer set up the ninth trick in dia-

monds, even if East has the ace. He will continue spades and you will lose 3 spade tricks and two aces. There is, of course, the heart finesse. If RHO has the $\heartsuit Q$, you can take nine tricks, ten if hearts are 3-3. So what's the big deal? Advice #1, Whenever you can safely run a long suit, do it!

Perhaps you do this automatically, but before taking the heart hook and crossing your fingers, run the clubs. You do this and LHO tosses the two, six and nine of diamonds and a heart. RHO follows to two more rounds and then pitches a diamond as well. For psychological effect, on the last club you discard a small heart from dummy. Maybe this works because righty lets go a heart. Well, what do you think? Is it possible that the hearts are now coming in?

You suspect LHO began with either 5341 or 5431 shape. With a fifth diamond, he may well have made a two-suited overcall of your weak no-trump opening. If lefty began with only three diamonds, then you can guarantee the contract with a throw-in, leading a spade now and waiting for a heart lead after West cashes his spades. But East's heart discard is screaming at you. Would RHO throw a heart from Qxx? Only if he is extremely talented. On the other hand, he may well have failed to appreciate the importance of the heart suit. Playing $\heartsuit A$, then $\heartsuit J$ from hand, you pick up the entire suit and make an overtrick, to boot. These were the hands:

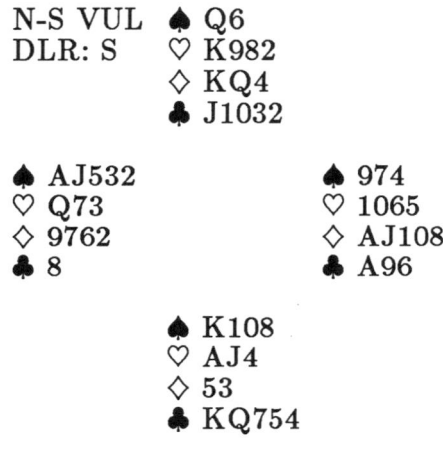

```
N-S VUL    ♠ Q6
DLR: S     ♡ K982
           ◇ KQ4
           ♣ J1032

♠ AJ532              ♠ 974
♡ Q73                ♡ 1065
◇ 9762               ◇ AJ108
♣ 8                  ♣ A96

           ♠ K108
           ♡ AJ4
           ◇ 53
           ♣ KQ754
```

Was this luck? Probably. A good defender in the East chair would have understood that only the diamond ace needed to be kept in that suit. But the point is that consistently providing defenders with the opportunity to go wrong is very good policy. In this case, the East defender was sloppy and failed to appreciate his partner's problem. His poor carding undid the beautiful job that West did, coming down to a doubleton heart queen and offering declarer a doomed throw-in.

Here's a hand from the Atlanta Fall Nationals:

```
ALL VUL  ♠ 832
DLR: S   ♡ 97
         ◇ 98
         ♣ AJ9853

         ♠ AKQ5
         ♡ A4
         ◇ KQ5
         ♣ Q1076
```

After a quick auction, South declared 3*NT*. Unfortunately, lefty had no problem finding his opening lead, the heart king. South ducked once and won the ♡*J* continuation. How would you proceed? The hand seems cut and dried. If the club finesse succeeds you have ten tricks. However, before taking that one chance run three spades. When you do this LHO discards a third round club deuce. You take a squirrely glance at your opponents' convention card but Hamman is not scrawled on the header. When you lead the club queen lefty continues with the four and you drop the stiff king offside. These were the hands:

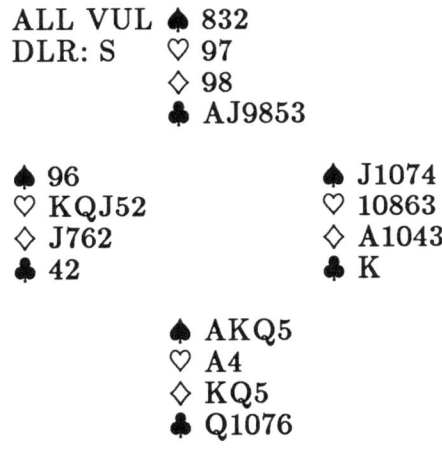

```
ALL VUL  ♠ 832
DLR: S   ♡ 97
         ◇ 98
         ♣ AJ9853

♠ 96              ♠ J1074
♡ KQJ52           ♡ 10863
◇ J762            ◇ A1043
♣ 42              ♣ K

         ♠ AKQ5
         ♡ A4
         ◇ KQ5
         ♣ Q1076
```

Why did you consult your opponent's convention card? If West had held king-third in clubs, only a club discard by him would have given you the opportunity to go wrong. But only a superb player would have deliberately made this play.

The same technique is not limited to the declaring side. Even when your tricks cannot go away, cashing the long suit on defense can give the declarer a nasty problem. Consider this example from the Kelsey classic, *More Killing Defense.*

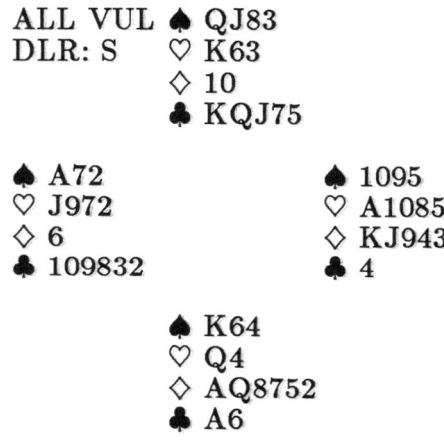

ALL VUL ♠ QJ83
DLR: S ♡ K63
◇ 10
♣ KQJ75

♠ A72   ♠ 1095
♡ J972   ♡ A1085
◇ 6   ◇ KJ943
♣ 109832   ♣ 4

♠ K64
♡ Q4
◇ AQ8752
♣ A6

The defense against South's 3*NT* contract begins with a heart to the ten and queen, followed by spades to the jack and back to the king and ace. If the defense cashes its three heart tricks now, declarer has to find a discard for dummy. It is likely he will bank on a reasonable club distribution and shed a spade from the board. Then a diamond return puts declarer to the brink. If he spurns the finesse, he goes down.

It is interesting to note that many of these *long* suits are actually quite modest in length, perhaps only four cards long as in the last example.

One reason why the technique of running a long suit is often overlooked is that the side with the long suit clearly appreciates where the problem is. It is sometimes difficult to remember that the other side is in the dark. Playing off length puts pressure to bear often before enough information is available to your opponents.

Here is a hand from the 1991 New York Goldman Pairs, a popular four-session event:

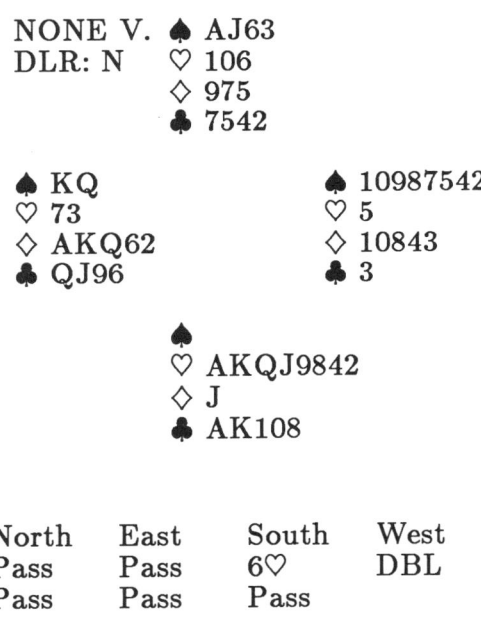

```
NONE V.    ♠ AJ63
DLR: N     ♡ 106
           ♢ 975
           ♣ 7542

♠ KQ                    ♠ 10987542
♡ 73                    ♡ 5
♢ AKQ62                 ♢ 10843
♣ QJ96                  ♣ 3

           ♠
           ♡ AKQJ9842
           ♢ J
           ♣ AK108
```

North	East	South	West
Pass	Pass	6♡	DBL
Pass	Pass	Pass	

Dispensing with scientific bidding, Linda Gordon opened the South hand at the six level and was promptly doubled. The defense began with two rounds of diamonds. After ruffing the second diamond with the eight, declarer considered her options. There are two *technical* lines. South can take a heart finesse and, should this hold, take a double finesse in clubs. If all goes well, she can enter the North hand with a second heart and repeat the club finesse. Gordon rejected this approach because of the double on her left. Curiously, the second, highly improbable, approach works. Take a heart finesse and play ace and a second spade hoping to find precisely king-queen doubleton with West.

Instead, declarer ran off all of her trumps. In the process, West believed that he was being squeezed in spades and clubs. Gambling that South held two cards in both black suits, he held on to the spades till the bitter end; a very bitter one at that.

There are three points to make here. First, one often prefers to run a long suit in preference to hoping for a remote but legitimate chance. Second, the spade holding in dummy had the appearance of being a threat. It is important to recognize and exploit apparent threats, even when you, as declarer, know that they are mirages. We shall see more of this in Chapter 9. Finally, this kind of disaster could have been avoided by cooperative defense. Instead of falling asleep from boredom, East should have discarded his club immediately, and then given proper count in spades.

Sometimes, you can improve the chances that an opponent will err in discarding by keeping his partner from helping him. This was a pretty hand played by Zia Mahmood:

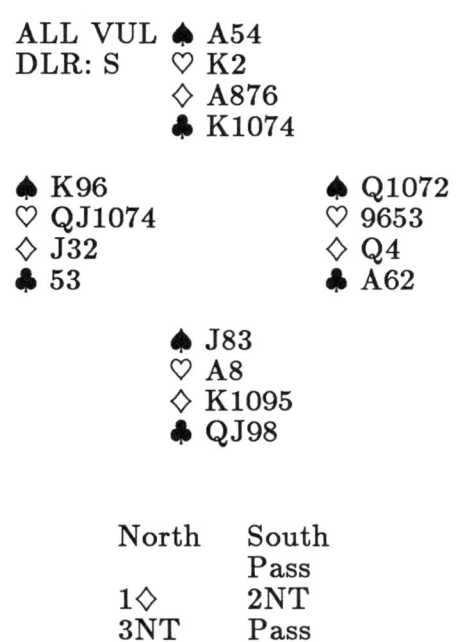

```
ALL VUL  ♠ A54
DLR: S   ♡ K2
         ◇ A876
         ♣ K1074

♠ K96              ♠ Q1072
♡ QJ1074           ♡ 9653
◇ J32              ◇ Q4
♣ 53               ♣ A62

         ♠ J83
         ♡ A8
         ◇ K1095
         ♣ QJ98
```

North	South
	Pass
1◇	2NT
3NT	Pass

Zia, South, received the ♡Q opening lead, and returned the club queen from hand. East won immediately and cleared hearts. The defenders now have four ready tricks, and it would seem that declarer must let them in with a diamond for a fifth. Again, with no other hope, it must be right to run the long suit.

On the second club, Zia unblocked the ten spot and continued with the eight at round three. The idea was to lead the last club through whichever defender had already discarded. In this way, one opponent would be forced to discard twice before his partner could make even one helpful discard. When West shook a spade on the third club, declarer ducked in dummy. This was the position with one club left to lead:

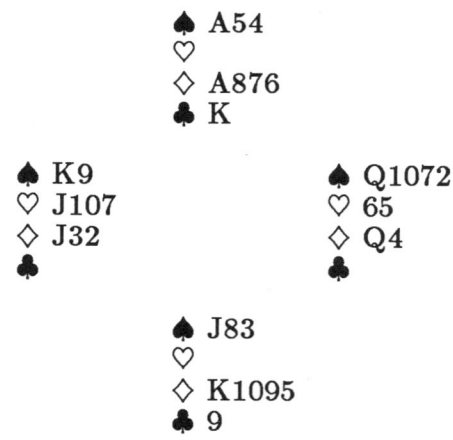

On the lead of the last club, West had to choose between baring his spade king and letting go a small diamond. When he did the latter, South had his ninth trick.

It is a well-known axiom that defenders must "keep length" with dummy. This is just a way of preventing declarer from establishing length winners. The same principle applies to length in declarer's own hand. Unfortunately for the defense, this side length is not always known.

When the auction concludes without exposing side length, running the trump suit will occasionally produce windfall profits. This is a good reason for not disclosing such assets. As a general rule, unscientific leaps to game will often make up in mis-defense what they risk in uncertainty.

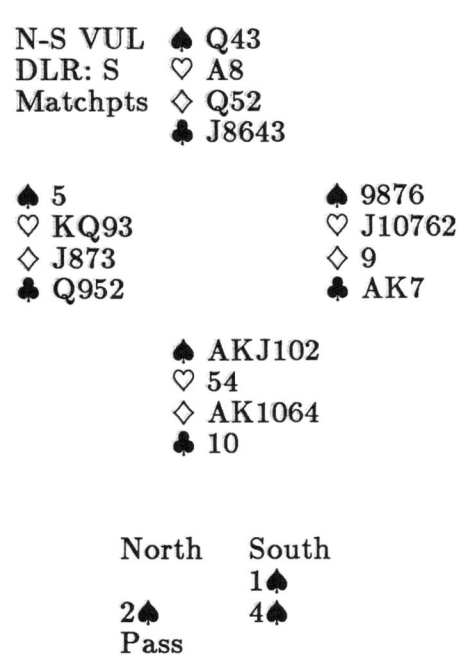

The opening lead of the king of hearts was ducked, East playing the jack, and hearts were continued. Two rounds of trumps disclosed the 4-1 break, and South continued spades.

Shortly this eight card end position was reached:

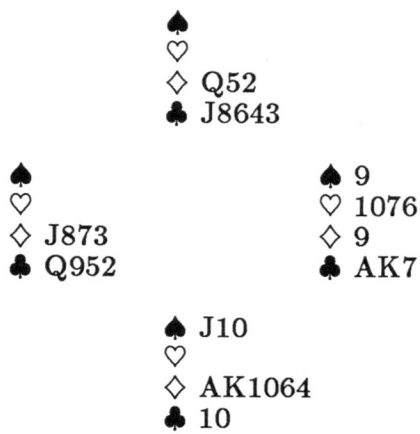

♠
♡
♦ Q52
♣ J8643

♠
♡
♦ J873
♣ Q952

♠ 9
♡ 1076
♦ 9
♣ AK7

♠ J10
♡
♦ AK1064
♣ 10

When the jack of spades was played from the South hand, West attempted to maintain length with dummy and shed a diamond, thus finishing off the defense. An interesting situation occurs if West sluffs a club at trick six. Then at matchpoints, declarer will have to decide whether to go for broke and play his last trump. If West can't stomach the thought of an unprotected queen he will rescue defeat from the jaws of victory.

As for the defense, East-West can solve this tricky problem if East plays spades up the line, suggesting club strength. Signalling strength in one suit by choice of carding is a thoughtful, expert technique.

Chapter 2
THE HIDDEN SIDE OF BRIDGE*

In Chapter 1, we saw that running a long suit can induce a careless, but informative discard by an opponent. Stick that one in your bag of tricks; it is probably the single most important tactic in the declarer *biz*. Furthermore, even when it doesn't work it is almost certain to drive the defenders batty and tire them out mentally – especially useful in team events.

This hand came from the Hartford (CT) regional, also. I particularly liked it because it was played against someone who finished 3rd/4th in the 1990 World Team championships in Geneva, Switzerland. OK. How do you create problems for even an international caliber player? Today's torture technique: *Keep the right cards concealed.*

You pick up in the South seat: ♠*K*103, ♡*Q*10763, ◇*Q*84, ♣92. Righty opens 1*NT* (10-12) and you are happy to pass. A glance at the board shows that you are vulnerable, so when LHO bids 2♡ to play, you grit your teeth and prepare to become partner's whipping boy. Sure enough, your MHO utters the ugly word DOUBLE, and pretty soon it's your turn.

The way you see it, there are two terrible options and a devious third one which is just as bad. The third one is to bid two spades – a call with so many things wrong with it, you quickly discard it. By the way, holding three spades is not a problem. Partner is sure to be aware that sometimes it's your best bid on three cards. It just won't occur to him that you have good defense

* In tribute to V. Mollo.

and fair values when you do it. So it comes down to a choice between pass and 2*NT*. Pass is really dangerous. Your hearts are too weak (partner could even be void), and the opponents cards lie in the right places, hearts behind you and points behind partner. Furthermore, much of the time you will set it for 100 or 300 and go back to compare against 600 or 630 your way.

You brace for disaster and bid 2*NT*. Lest you think this is a painless bid, think again. For one, it has too wide a range. At IMPS, vulnerable, partner is likely to stretch for a game, especially when the opponents have described their hands so thoroughly. Furthermore, unlike spades which are unlikely to get doubled, LHO can easily evaluate his side's total points and double 3*NT* when it's right. Your teammates are just as unlikely to appreciate -500 opposite a part score as they are a missed game. Back to real life, partner stretches to 3*NT* and lefty internationalist doubles. He leads the ♡2 and watches while you choke on dummy.

```
N-S VUL    ♠ QJ64
DLR: E     ♡ 9
           ♢ AK72
           ♣ A864



           ♠ K103
           ♡ Q10763
           ♢ Q84
           ♣ 92
```

The best thing you can say is that these are *noisy* hands. Whenever there is a lot of junk – scattered values – hanging around, the defense has to be careful not to drop tricks by being too active. That's good; everything else about the contract stinks!

Well, RHO wins the ace and returns the ♡8 which is break number one. You are going to cover this card, but for psychological reasons you play the *Q*. After all, you do want a heart return. However, this kind of play doesn't get one to Geneva. A switch is in order, but to what suit? You hold your breath and count to -800 for practice. When you look down a small diamond is on the table, break number two. It is time to think long and hard.

What are your chances? You can set up spades now for 3 tricks. This plus three diamonds plus the ace of clubs gets you up to -500. If the diamonds are 3-3 you're at -200. Should you cash out? Not really. The diamonds are likely to be 4-2. Furthermore, your partners could well defend 1*NT* or 2♠. In that case you are going to generate a 7-10 IMP loss anyway. Well, back to the diamond return. Why didn't LHO table a club? He certainly would have if he held two club honors. On the other hand, if RHO held all three club honors, he may well have shifted to clubs at trick two. Hence, you are going to play West for a club honor, probably the *K*. That leaves all the unaccounted honor cards in East's hand.

What do the opponents know? Lefty doesn't know who has the ◇*Q*. After all, your diamond queen could easily be the club honor instead. Righty doesn't know how many spade tricks you are entitled to. It's crucial to take advantage of both of these, but especially the

$\diamondsuit Q$. Once LHO knows that you have that card, the club honors will be marked.

So you win in dummy with the $\diamondsuit K$ and lead a low spade off the board. From righty's perspective you may be missing the $\spadesuit 10$. If he hops with the ace you will have three tricks instead of two in the suit, so you win the ten. Why the ten? You are done fooling RHO, but it's just possible that East ducked from $\spadesuit AKxx$. Again, this would be necessary to hold declarer to one spade trick when he holds $10xx$. Done with righty, it's time to turn the screws on lefty. Instead of continuing spades, you switch back to hearts, leading the 10. What will West do? Quickly it is all over. He wins the heart and returns.... a diamond! You win in hand, cash out hearts and establish the spades for nine tricks. The defenders have taken three hearts, and a spade. 750 is a nice number, and so is the 12 IMPS.

The full hands:

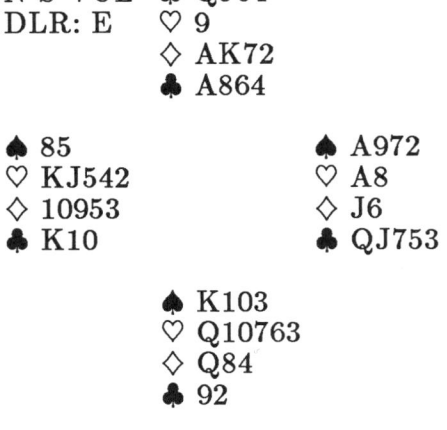

```
N-S VUL    ♠ QJ64
DLR: E     ♡ 9
           ♢ AK72
           ♣ A864

♠ 85              ♠ A972
♡ KJ542           ♡ A8
♢ 10953           ♢ J6
♣ K10             ♣ QJ753

           ♠ K103
           ♡ Q10763
           ♢ Q84
           ♣ 92
```

A moral, right? Every bridge hand has a tale to tell. Well two things spring to mind. If you play the $\diamond Q$ at trick 3 you are 99% *bona fide* certain to go down. And what the opponents don't know about your hands can certainly hurt them.

A major advantage which declarer always has is a complete knowledge of the honors his side is missing. On the other hand, defenders only know roughly the point range that declarer should have. We saw this disadvantage exploited to the extreme on the last hand. There it was necessary for East-West to find an active defense and they didn't know where to strike. On the other hand, sometimes a passive defense is the best hope for the defenders. If that is the case, it is frequently crucial to *mask* the location of high cards.

Suppose you open the bidding, sitting East, with a weak 2♠. The opponents get to 4♡, and your partner leads the two of spades, indicating a three card holding. What do you play from ♠AKQ754 if two spades appear in dummy?

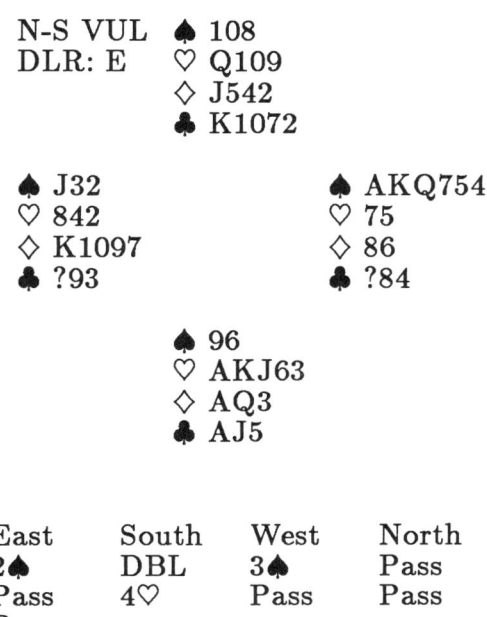

```
              N-S VUL    ♠ 108
              DLR: E     ♡ Q109
                         ◇ J542
                         ♣ K1072

         ♠ J32                    ♠ AKQ754
         ♡ 842                    ♡ 75
         ◇ K1097                  ◇ 86
         ♣ ?93                    ♣ ?84

                    ♠ 96
                    ♡ AKJ63
                    ◇ AQ3
                    ♣ AJ5
```

East	South	West	North
2♠	DBL	3♠	Pass
Pass	4♡	Pass	Pass
Pass			

The answer depends, in fact, on the question marks. If you hold the queen of clubs, you must play the queen of spades. Some people would open the East hand 1♠ on your eleven count. This may be just the small *advantage* South is looking for to finesse the wrong way in the club suit. On the other hand, if you do not hold the club queen, play the king of spades to trick one. This will allow declarer the chance to find *more* points in your hand.

A full discussion of masking cannot be dealt with here, because this would carry us into the province of false carding, an enormous subject which has been considered extensively elsewhere. Defenders will often mask cards in order to "build a fence" around partner. Here we are only concerned with masking that leads to errors in judgment on the part of the opponents.

There is a not so well-known "Rule of seven" in no-trump play. When the opponents have attacked your weak suit, and you can afford to let them hold the lead, subtract the total number of cards you hold in both hands from seven. The difference is the number of times you should hold up before winning. If you are blessed with more than one stopper in the weak suit, then you can hold up one less time for each additional stopper. Wow! Here is an illustration.

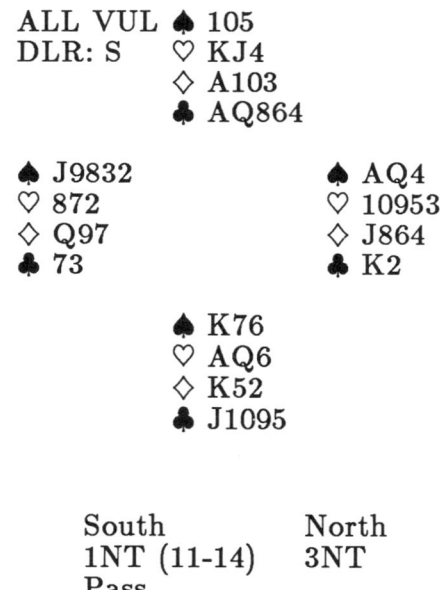

```
ALL VUL  ♠ 105
DLR: S   ♡ KJ4
         ♢ A103
         ♣ AQ864

♠ J9832              ♠ AQ4
♡ 872                ♡ 10953
♢ Q97                ♢ J864
♣ 73                 ♣ K2

         ♠ K76
         ♡ AQ6
         ♢ K52
         ♣ J1095
```

```
South        North
1NT (11-14)  3NT
Pass
```

When West starts the three of spades against the North-South no-trump game, East might insert the ace. Since South has one spade stopper, he applies the rule of seven as follows. Seven minus the number of spades

24

he owns in both hands, $7 - 5$, equals two, so he holds up twice winning the third spade with the king. The ♣K is the last trick for defense.

Of course, the ♠A was the wrong card to play at trick one for East. If he plays the queen, South cannot be sure that he has a stopper in the suit. To cater to the possibility that West began with AJ—fifth in the spade suit, South must win the first spade. When the club finesse loses, the defenders easily take five tricks to defeat the contract. This is a well-known sequence for East. In a way, though, South has not erred; East's proper play of the queen almost forces him to go wrong.

On the other hand, occasionally, a declarer will get sloppy if he thinks he is out of danger. Greed at match points can be just the tonic to encourage a misplay. Consider a slightly altered deal.

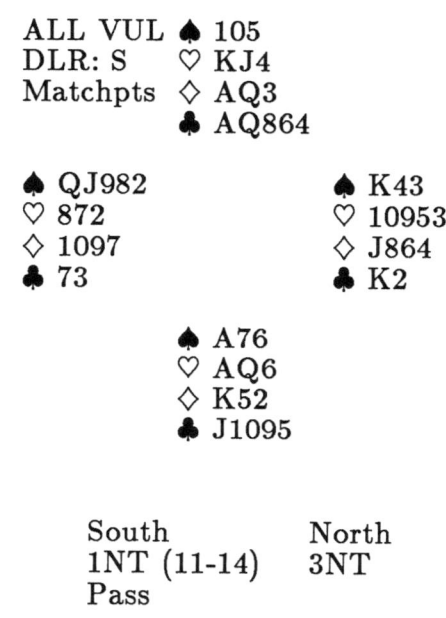

ALL VUL ♠ 105
DLR: S ♡ KJ4
Matchpts ♢ AQ3
♣ AQ864

♠ QJ982   ♠ K43
♡ 872   ♡ 10953
♢ 1097   ♢ J864
♣ 73   ♣ K2

♠ A76
♡ AQ6
♢ K52
♣ J1095

South   North
1NT (11-14)   3NT
Pass

On the lead of the queen of spades, East inserts the *king*. He can do this safely because West will generally lead low from *QJ*— fifth holdings, except *QJ*10 and *QJ*9. The play of the king is the normal play from king and one. If South thinks the spades are divided 6-2, he will forsake the rule of seven and win the ace on the second round. Instead of an overtrick, an undertrick will greet him.

Masking is a useful device for declarer as well. The most common situations involve what appear to be finessible tenaces. Consider the following defensive problem:

```
ALL VUL    ♠ 753
DLR: S     ♡ AQ84
Matchpts   ◇ J53
           ♣ QJ6

♠ J8642
♡ 93
◇ AQ64
♣ K4
```

	South	North
	-------	-------
	1NT	2♣
	2◇	3NT
	Pass	

After your opening lead of the four of spades, declarer wins in hand, heading your partner's queen with the ace. At trick two, he leads a heart to the ace and runs the club queen. What do you return?

If you have a suspicious mind, you may well return a diamond. You will be right if this is the layout.

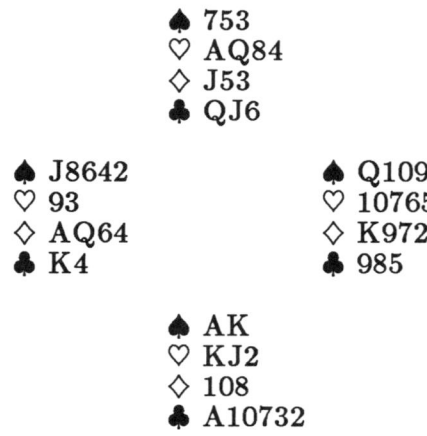

On the other hand, declarer might play the same way with each of the following two holdings:

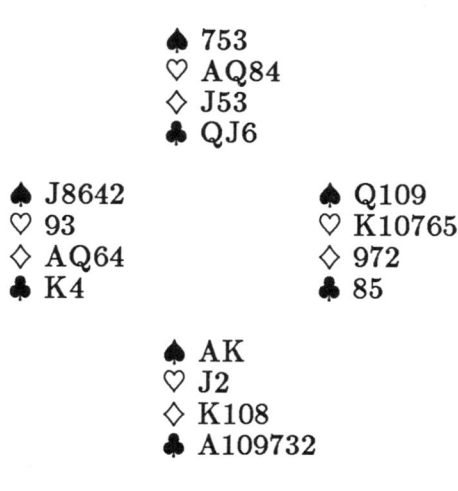

or:

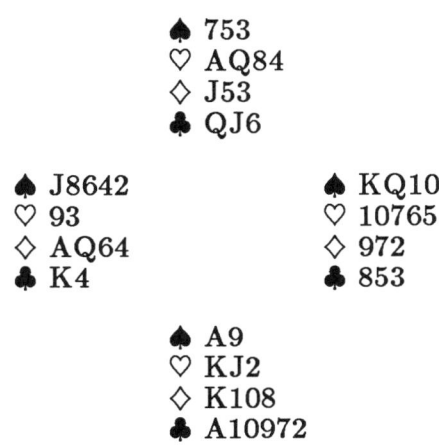

♠ 753
♥ AQ84
♦ J53
♣ QJ6

♠ J8642   ♠ KQ10
♥ 93   ♥ 10765
♦ AQ64   ♦ 972
♣ K4   ♣ 853

♠ A9
♥ KJ2
♦ K108
♣ A10972

The point is that in all cases, declarer should enter
dummy with the ace. With the first and third holdings
leading a heart to the queen would be a foolish play. It
would announce to West, the *danger* hand, that South
had the king of hearts. Declarer would reduce the number of ways by which you could go wrong.

Incidentally, many defenders now signal high or low
in the side suits (hearts and clubs in this last example) to indicate interest or disinterest in the initial suit
(spades). A high heart and a high club by East in the
last example would help West to continue spades.

When RHO is the danger hand, the opposite ploy is sometimes your best chance.

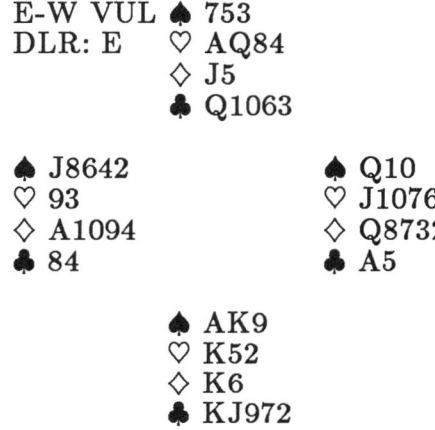

E-W VUL ♠ 753
DLR: E   ♡ AQ84
         ◇ J5
         ♣ Q1063

♠ J8642   ♠ Q10
♡ 93   ♡ J1076
◇ A1094   ◇ Q8732
♣ 84   ♣ A5

         ♠ AK9
         ♡ K52
         ◇ K6
         ♣ KJ972

After a similar auction, North-South get to 3*NT*. West again begins the four of spades. South wins this trick, enters dummy with a heart to the *queen* and returns a low club to the king. When this wins, declarer continues clubs to the ten and ace. At this point, East may not perceive the need to return a diamond and put declarer to a guess. If he places the king of hearts with West, then a lead away from the diamond queen would appear to cost a trick.

The play in no-trump often resembles a 100-yard dash, with each side rushing to establish its source of tricks first. Therefore, a ready conclusion most defenders make is that if declarer doesn't touch a long, broken suit in dummy he has the filling honors in hand. To distract the defenders, the declarer can sometimes exploit an apparent finesse. For example,

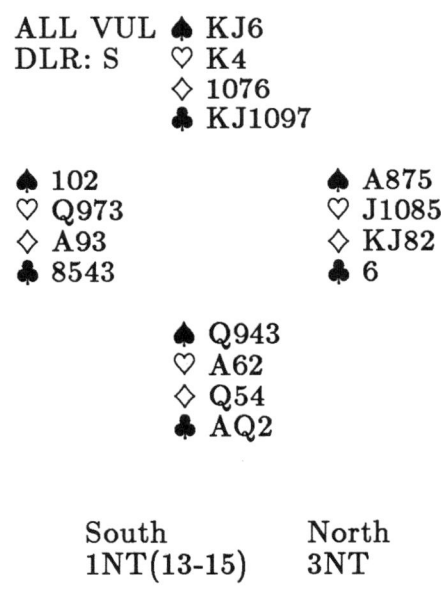

```
ALL VUL  ♠ KJ6
DLR: S   ♡ K4
         ◇ 1076
         ♣ KJ1097

♠ 102            ♠ A875
♡ Q973           ♡ J1085
◇ A93            ◇ KJ82
♣ 8543           ♣ 6

         ♠ Q943
         ♡ A62
         ◇ Q54
         ♣ AQ2


South        North
1NT(13-15)   3NT
```

If declarer wins the opening lead of the three of hearts in dummy and proceeds with spades, East will tentatively assign him five club tricks. He might well find the killing shift to the jack of diamonds. But if declarer wins the first trick with the ace and takes the club "finesse", East is less likely to place the cards and find the diamond shift when he subsequently wins the ace of spades.

Since competent defenders will watch for a failure to attack dummy's long suit, it is your duty to *attempt to establish* solid suits when a switch would be deadly. How do you play the following 3NT contract, adapted from a Mollo defensive quiz? Assume West begins the queen of clubs and East follows with the three (showing an odd number).

♠ Q76
♡ J93
♢ KQ876
♣ K4

♠ AJ85
♡ 864
♢ A43
♣ A52

South	North
1NT(13-15)	3NT

You should win the club in hand with the ace and lead the diamond three to the board's queen. When this holds, return a spade to the jack. If West wins with the king, he may place his partner with the ace of diamonds. It would, of course, have been good defense for West to have ducked smoothly from ace and one. With that assumption, West would certainly continue the attack on clubs. The full diagram:

$$\spadesuit \text{ Q76}$$
$$\heartsuit \text{ J93}$$
$$\diamondsuit \text{ KQ876}$$
$$\clubsuit \text{ K4}$$

♠ K103	♠ 942
♡ Q10	♡ AK752
◇ J52	◇ 109
♣ QJ1098	♣ 763

$$\spadesuit \text{ AJ85}$$
$$\heartsuit \text{ 864}$$
$$\diamondsuit \text{ A43}$$
$$\clubsuit \text{ A52}$$

Would West really find the heart switch if you win in dummy and take an immediate finesse? He should if he is counting; he will place you with the diamond, spade and club aces, as well as the spade jack.

Hands requiring a hold-up are well-known. There are other hands where a hold-up is deadly, not because a shift will be inconvenient, but rather because a continuation will expose weakness. Consider this matrix in a no-trump contract:

$$\heartsuit \text{ 65}$$

$$\heartsuit \text{ A2}$$

Unless you win an opening heart lead confidently with the ace, the defenders will be certain to continue. If other traps lie about, you may be able to *freeze* the defense long enough to make your contract. Here is a hand from a local team event:

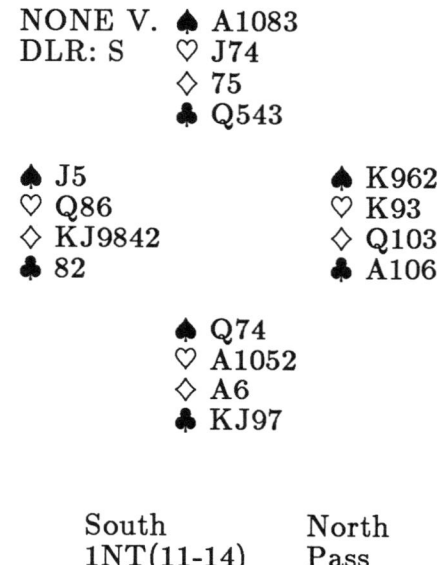

```
NONE V.   ♠ A1083
DLR: S    ♡ J74
          ◇ 75
          ♣ Q543

♠ J5              ♠ K962
♡ Q86             ♡ K93
◇ KJ9842          ◇ Q103
♣ 82              ♣ A106

          ♠ Q74
          ♡ A1052
          ◇ A6
          ♣ KJ97
```

South	North
1NT(11-14)	Pass

The opening lead was the eight of diamonds, leaving South with a problem. However, without pausing, South won the opening lead and confidently *finessed* the queen of spades. East held up his king and the declarer, switched to clubs making his contract.

If you put the defense to the critical guess early, they will have to rely on inference to know how to proceed. In standard carding methods, this inference is more likely to come from declarer play than from the defenders' own carding technique. A famous example of this is the "winner on loser" play.

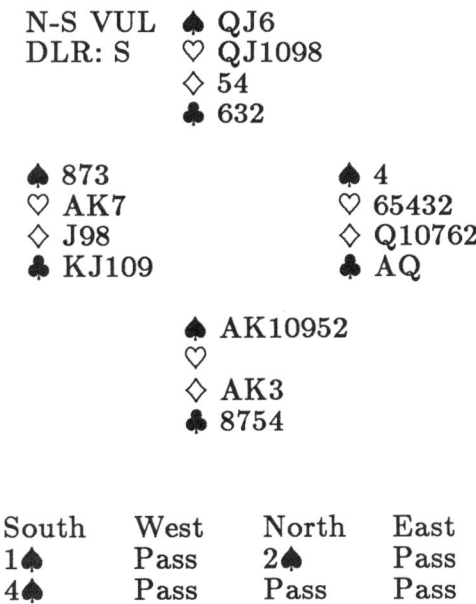

```
N-S VUL    ♠ QJ6
DLR: S     ♡ QJ1098
           ◇ 54
           ♣ 632

♠ 873              ♠ 4
♡ AK7              ♡ 65432
◇ J98              ◇ Q10762
♣ KJ109            ♣ AQ

           ♠ AK10952
           ♡
           ◇ AK3
           ♣ 8754
```

South	West	North	East
1♠	Pass	2♠	Pass
4♠	Pass	Pass	Pass

Unfortunately for the defense, West began with the heart king, ruffed in the closed hand. Since a signal from East might prove deadly, South led only one round of trumps, low to dummy's queen, before continuing hearts. On the second round of that suit, he discarded the three of diamonds. When West came in, it seemed natural to switch to diamonds. South gratefully won, pulled trump, and threw away three losing clubs on the remaining hearts. The only losers for declarer were a club and a heart. Of course, there is scope for double bluff in this example. West will wonder why South has not pulled a second round of trumps before establishing the heart suit. If he knows about the nefarious ways of the declarer, a club discard may be best anyway. Being the suspicious sort, his diamond return will again result in eleven tricks. This kind of result can be avoided if East is careful to make suit preference plays on the first two hearts, playing the two and then the three. However, he must guess that a club switch is better than a diamond switch, not at all clear on the bidding.

Since a discard by declarer is frequently the only help given to the defenders, it should affect the choice of which loser to get rid of. Here is a hand played by Henry Bethe on his way to winning the North American Open Pairs in the Atlantic City 1991 Nationals:

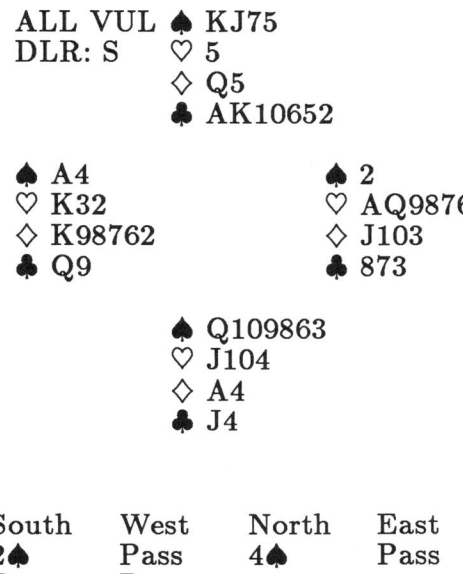

ALL VUL ♠ KJ75
DLR: S ♡ 5
◇ Q5
♣ AK10652

♠ A4   ♠ 2
♡ K32   ♡ AQ9876
◇ K98762   ◇ J103
♣ Q9   ♣ 873

♠ Q109863
♡ J104
◇ A4
♣ J4

South	West	North	East
2♠	Pass	4♠	Pass
Pass	Pass		

With the little information afforded by the bidding,
West selected the opening lead of the club queen. Bethe
won in dummy, played one round of spades, ducked by
West and then switched back to clubs throwing a diamond on the third round. When West ruffed with the
ace, he had to guess which suit to switch to and chose
diamonds. This allowed Bethe to take all the remaining tricks. Here, East is entirely to blame. His first club
cards should have been the eight and the seven, alerting
his partner to the location of the heart ace.

As we have noted before, the theme of the book
is to create problems for the opponents, not to solve
them. Even in the finals of a national championship,
errors dominate the picture and eliciting them from your
opponents will be the difference.

Chapter 3
RUFF STUFF

Some impediments, roadblocks and flak work best when tossed at bad or careless players. That doesn't mean you shouldn't keep in practice by harassing the pros as well. It's just that they will more often easily sidestep your projectiles. Concealment, as we have seen last time, can be effective against even the best players. On the other hand, offering up free ruffs is unlikely to get you rich in the Blue Ribbons, but it is a great Open Pairs device for stealing chunks of match points.

The way it works is as follows. Say you are down to this four card ending:

♠ A
♡ AJ7
◇
♣

♠
♡ K103
◇ A
♣

Hearts are trump and five are out to the ♡Q. Additionally, righty's out of spades, but not lefty. Clearly, all you care about is the trump lady. It's only a matter of guessing which way to play the hearts, and it can hardly matter which of the aces you score up for your other trick. Nevertheless, before playing a trump, for maximum confusion, lead the spade. Now, "dare ain't no guarantees", as they say in Brooklyn, but RHO looking at a couple of small trumps may well ruff. On the other hand, the same player is unlikely to trump with Qxx, and certainly won't ruff low with Q and one. (Occasionally he may try to promote a trick for partner by trumping with the Q!) If there is a small chance that RHO will succumb, the odds for picking up the suit change markedly, in your favor.

Now let's see a similar seduction in the context of a complete deal. You arrive in 4♠, West leads the ♠9, and you are not thrilled with your chances.

```
NONE V.   ♠ 874
DLR: S    ♡ J7653
          ♢ AK5
          ♣ 64

♠ 92              ♠ J106
♡ Q8              ♡ K104
♢ J9763           ♢ Q10842
♣ A752            ♣ K3

          ♠ AKQ53
          ♡ A92
          ♢
          ♣ QJ1098
```

There seems to be a little problem. You have nine tricks in your hand and two on the board, but, to put it cutely, North and South aren't speaking to each other. How do you rectify the problem? You simply enlist unrestrained greed on the part of your opponents. At trick two, fire out the ♣Q. If you have an eager East, the play may go: ♣K, ♣3, club ruff. Now you politely win the heart return, draw the last trump and sacrifice another club winner to dummy's last trump. After two dis-heart-ening discards on the $\diamond AK$ your hand is up. You have collapsed 4 club winners into 2 but made your contract. If instead, RHO had allowed your third club to win, you would have found yourself with only nine tricks. *C'est la vie.*

Of course, the really enjoyable part of this hand comes when East **pounces** on the $\clubsuit K$ to get his ruff. Definitely much more enjoyable than the opponent who tentatively wins the club and returns another with no certainty. Havoc tastes much better when spiced with his ultimate chagrin!

It is seldom correct to ruff one of declarer's losers. This does not mean, however, that your opponents know this. If you have neglected to play off all of your high trumps, a defender may not even recognize that he holds a master card. In the following deal, North-South have an "accident" and miss their 4-4 heart fit, playing, instead, 4♠.

```
N-S VUL   ♠ K75
DLR: N    ♡ 6543
          ♢ AQ8
          ♣ Q64

          ♠ A10984
          ♡ AK72
          ♢ K62
          ♣ 7
```

The opening lead is the Rusinow ♡J, indicating the queen or shortness, and South wins and leads a spade to the king. Once on the board, however, declarer continues with the heart five, two of spades, heart two and eight. East returns the ♣10 and West wins and gives his partner yet another heart ruff, but the hand is over. Declarer wins the return, pulls the remaining trump and claims. He has lost two heart ruffs and the ace of clubs. Here is the full deal:

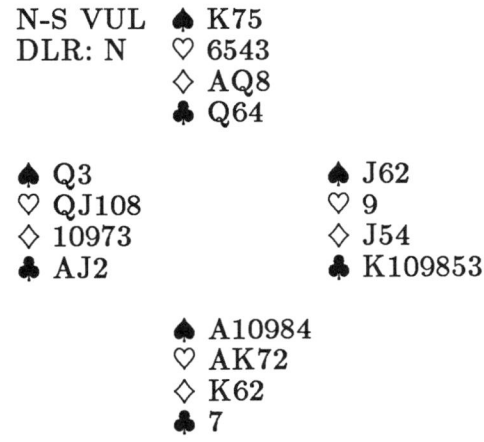

```
N-S VUL    ♠ K75
DLR: N     ♡ 6543
           ◇ AQ8
           ♣ Q64

♠ Q3                    ♠ J62
♡ QJ108                 ♡ 9
◇ 10973                 ◇ J54
♣ AJ2                   ♣ K109853

           ♠ A10984
           ♡ AK72
           ◇ K62
           ♣ 7
```

There are two interesting points to note about this hand. With hearts 4-1, South needed a singleton spade honor in the West hand in order to have a legitimate chance for the game. (With both spade honors in the West hand, declarer would probably rely on restricted choice and go down one.) Once his left hand opponent failed to follow high to the spade trick, the only possibility was to enlist RHO in a "loser-on-loser" play. The opportunity to get two heart ruffs was more than East could refuse.

Now consider a nearly identical problem.

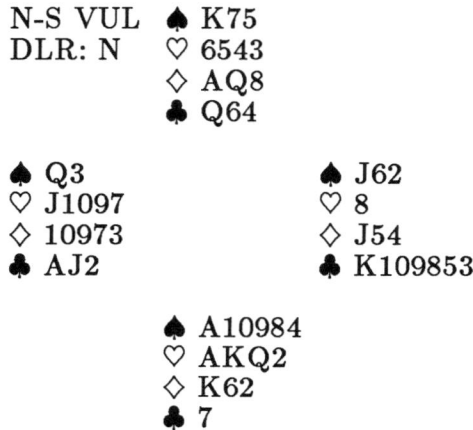

```
N-S VUL    ♠ K75
DLR: N     ♡ 6543
           ◇ AQ8
           ♣ Q64

♠ Q3              ♠ J62
♡ J1097           ♡ 8
◇ 10973           ◇ J54
♣ AJ2             ♣ K109853

           ♠ A10984
           ♡ AKQ2
           ◇ K62
           ♣ 7
```

In this version, declarer finds himself in 5♠, and the opening lead is the heart jack. Now, South must employ the *Scissors Coup*, leading a low club from hand at trick two. Ideal from declarer's perspective would be for West to rise with the ace and lead another heart for East to ruff. If instead, East tops the club queen with his king, South can trump the club continuation, enter dummy with a spade to the king, and lead a heart from the board, offering East his "chance."

In the last two examples, one defender was ruffing with natural trump winners, but he did not realize this at the time. In the following, admittedly bizarre, example from a Sectional tournament, East needed to keep a losing trump card as a sort of place-holder. Many errors were needed to permit the following disaster, but the worst was the hardest to spot.

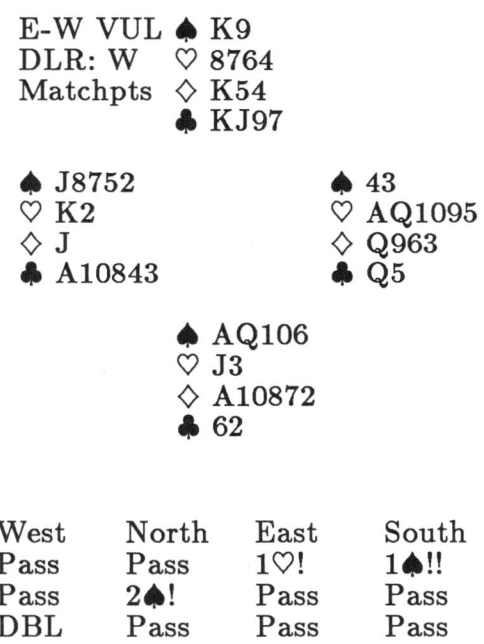

```
E-W VUL  ♠ K9
DLR: W   ♡ 8764
Matchpts ♢ K54
         ♣ KJ97

♠ J8752          ♠ 43
♡ K2             ♡ AQ1095
♢ J              ♢ Q963
♣ A10843         ♣ Q5

         ♠ AQ106
         ♡ J3
         ♢ A10872
         ♣ 62
```

West	North	East	South
Pass	Pass	1♡!	1♠!!
Pass	2♠!	Pass	Pass
DBL	Pass	Pass	Pass

After an aggressive auction, South found himself declaring a rather tenuous contract. While 2♡ was likely to be made, 3♢ with the North-South hands might also make. The prospects for a good matchpoint score were slim, even if declarer could salvage -100. However, the defense was amply generous. West began with the king of hearts to which East would only contribute the five.

At trick two, West switched to the ace and then continued with a club, perhaps trying to give East a ruff.

In with the club king, and noting the drop of the queen from East, declarer laid a small trap. At trick four he continued with the club nine. Perhaps fearing that South was hoping to sneak a club by him, East ruffed with the three. South over-ruffed with the *ten*, finessed the nine of spades, and played the jack of clubs pitching his last heart. Since East had wasted one of his trumps ruffing South's losing club he could no longer interfere. The rest of the hand went quickly, heart ruff, diamond to the king, heart ruff, and South had the spade king left for his eighth trick. Of course, North remarked how unlucky declarer was to lose the diamond ace to a ruff.

On the serious side, as bad as this defensive effort was, bear in mind that defenders below the level of Flight A routinely make errors of this sort at trump contracts. They allow declarer to tap himself when they own a source of tricks, and they ruff frequently with apparently worthless small trump. We shall see some more examples later. The key from declarer's point of view is to leave destructive options always open to the defenders. This is a constant repetitive message, not just in this Chapter, but throughout the book.

Sometimes, when left to his own devices, a defender will find a *natural* switch to a trump, especially at times inconvenient to you, the declarer. This is frequently the case when you appear to be interested in ruffing losers. Occasionally you can seduce a defender into returning to his original defensive plan. If that plan was to get a ruff, why not offer one up?!

```
N-S VUL    ♠ A10743
DLR: S     ♡ J93
           ◇ 752
           ♣ 65

♠ 5                    ♠ QJ98
♡ 104                  ♡ 852
◇ J8643                ◇ KQ109
♣ AQ1074               ♣ 93

           ♠ K62
           ♡ AKQ76
           ◇ A
           ♣ KJ82
```

South	West	North	East
1♡	2NT*	Pass	3◇
4◇	Pass	4♡	Pass
Pass	Pass		

*=both minors

After a spirited auction, LHO decides to lead a singleton-looking spade. Since West is likely to have one or both club honors, an immediate club switch might well result in his sudden interest in a more successful defense- namely leading trumps. In order to keep your opponent "on track" you should win the opening lead in your hand and continue spades at trick two. If West is surprised and grateful, he will win your offering and the defense will be over. It will now be impossible to prevent you from ruffing two clubs in dummy.

The logical converse of the previous approach, getting your opponents to attack trumps for you, has a limited applicability.

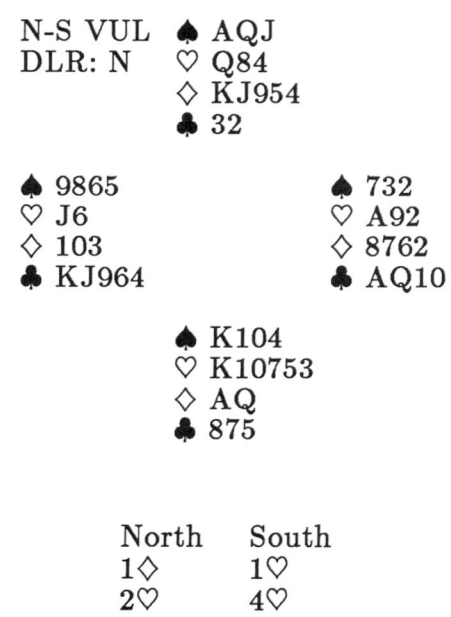

```
N-S VUL    ♠ AQJ
DLR: N     ♡ Q84
           ◇ KJ954
           ♣ 32

♠ 9865              ♠ 732
♡ J6                ♡ A92
◇ 103               ◇ 8762
♣ KJ964             ♣ AQ10

           ♠ K104
           ♡ K10753
           ◇ AQ
           ♣ 875
```

North	South
1◇	1♡
2♡	4♡

After bidding to a heart game, you receive the lead of the nine of spades. While there are several possible ways to play the contract, winning in dummy and leading the club deuce may get East to win the trick and switch to trumps in order to "cut down" your club ruffs.

Inexperienced players often underestimate the value of trump length, especially when these are *losers*. If you are declaring a contract where trump control will ultimately become a problem, offering a loser-on-loser play early on in the hand is best. This was a hand from a Pennsylvania sectional tournament:

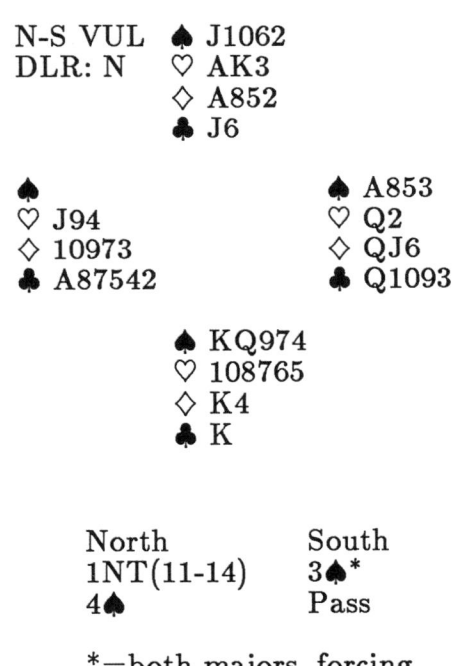

```
N-S VUL    ♠ J1062
DLR: N     ♡ AK3
           ◇ A852
           ♣ J6

♠                      ♠ A853
♡ J94                  ♡ Q2
◇ 10973                ◇ QJ6
♣ A87542               ♣ Q1093

           ♠ KQ974
           ♡ 108765
           ◇ K4
           ♣ K
```

North	South
1NT(11-14)	3♠*
4♠	Pass

*=both majors, forcing.

After aggressive bidding by declarer, West started the ♣A and another, ruffed in hand. The play continued, king of spades, West showing out and East ducking, heart to the king, and ace of hearts. On the lead of the last heart from dummy, East ruffed, allowing South to make his contract. This was a fundamentally wrong play because it could not gain a trick, even when West did not hold the winner.

As the cards lie, East would have defeated the contract by holding onto his small trump. When West gets in with the heart jack, he continues the club suit, allowing South a useless ruff and discard. Later on, East will have the opportunity to score a small ruff, or will win the trump ace and continue clubs after one hand no longer has any trumps remaining. In either case, declarer will find himself a trick shy.

Chapter 4
QUICK DRAW MC GUESS

As you will by now have noticed, some of the techniques we've examined in the first three chapters worked best against weaker players, perhaps not at all against strong opponents. The reason they failed is that very good players do two things much more consistently and accurately. They keep track of the cards played, and they draw the proper conclusions from what they've seen.

A little thought will indicate that there is a time element involved in this skill. For example, suppose that you have to make a critical play, say, whether to hold up or win at trick two. You've heard the bidding, seen the opening trick and the remaining cards in dummy and your hand, and then perhaps as much as two more cards. Now there are certain to be plenty of inferences available from all of this to help you, but the fact remains that there are still 22 unknown cards held by partner and declarer. On the other hand, which card to discard at trick 11 is a decision you'll face with only four or five missing cards and plenty of signals exchanged between you and partner – legal ones, of course.

What all of this argues for is simply: make the critical defensive problem occur as soon as possible. Consider this hand:

♠ AJ43
♡ A2
◇ J104
♣ 9852

♠ KQ6
♡ K93
◇ 75
♣ AQ1063

In a moment of matchpoint greed you fire off a 1NT salvo in third seat with the south hand. Unfortunately, your partner can add 15 and 10 and so, after duly invoking Stayman, he places you in the precarious contract of 3NT. Why is your partner beaming at you? He has just figured out that an average score on the last board will salt away the win. What could be more ordinary than 3NT on 25 points and two balanced hands?

However all is not lost, for lefty has tabled a low heart. There are two things good about a low heart. One is that it ain't a diamond. The other is that it doesn't tell RHO what high heart is where.

Since you have read Chapter 2, you know that it will be important to conceal the ♡K on this hand. The dictum of this chapter tells you not to hold up in hearts either. Why not? Well, if you win the second heart, RHO's return might tell West who has the heart king; and, of course, East might switch to diamonds for an immediate set. (Going down fast never has had much appeal.)

So you win the ♡A on the board and try an immediate finesse of the ♣Q. Unfortunately, lefty has the ♣K, but without thinking too much he tables a heart.

Now, it's true that you might still guess wrong at clubs, but this time Providence gave West only two chances to set the contract, and you make 10 tricks for 630 and a top. As you walk to the scorer's table you notice that partner has stopped a step or two behind. Strangely, he seems to be doing some mental calculation. Bizarre fellow, that one.

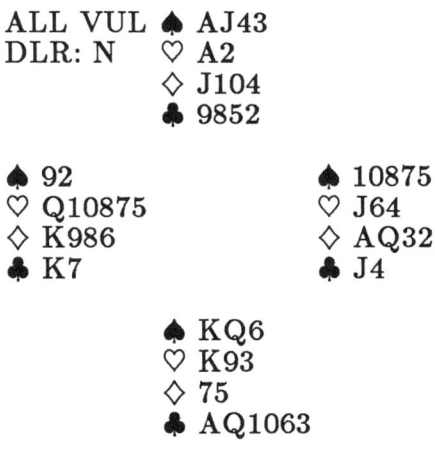

```
ALL VUL   ♠ AJ43
DLR: N    ♡ A2
          ◇ J104
          ♣ 9852

♠ 92              ♠ 10875
♡ Q10875          ♡ J64
◇ K986            ◇ AQ32
♣ K7              ♣ J4

          ♠ KQ6
          ♡ K93
          ◇ 75
          ♣ AQ1063
```

Much of the material covered throughout this book has to do with timing. In some cases, a declarer who needs help from the opponents must delay his critical action until the opponents have had a chance to err, perhaps by too informative a discard or carelessly ruffing (see the previous Chapter). When the goal is to hide important information from the opponents, the opposite is true. Allowing time for the defenders to help each other will be fatal. It is often the case, when declaring, that you must take a dangerous line in order to avoid letting the defense find a discard:

```
N-S VUL   ♠ J63
DLR: S    ♡ AQ106
          ◇ 874
          ♣ 652

♠ K95              ♠ 872
♡ 854              ♡ 97
◇ J963             ◇ Q1052
♣ K87              ♣ AQ94

          ♠ AQ104
          ♡ KJ32
          ◇ AK
          ♣ J103
```

South	West	North	East
1♡	Pass	3♡*	Pass
4♡	Pass	Pass	Pass

*=semi-preemptive, 5-8 points with good 4-card trump support.

The opening lead is the 6◇ headed by the queen and the *ace*. Declarer clearly cannot let E-W find their club winners so he must go to dummy in trumps, draw only one more round, and then take the spade finesse with one trump outstanding. West can throw a monkey wrench into the works by holding off. Now, if declarer finishes trumps before repeating the hook, East will have a chance to signal in clubs. Should West win immediately he will have to guess whether to continue diamonds or to switch. Perhaps half the time he will go wrong.

Another way of looking at this motif is that the pressure faced by the defenders is greatly increased when they must make decisions early on in the play of the hand. On rare occasions it may even be more reasonable to play for a defensive error than to take another line with a better *technical* chance of success.

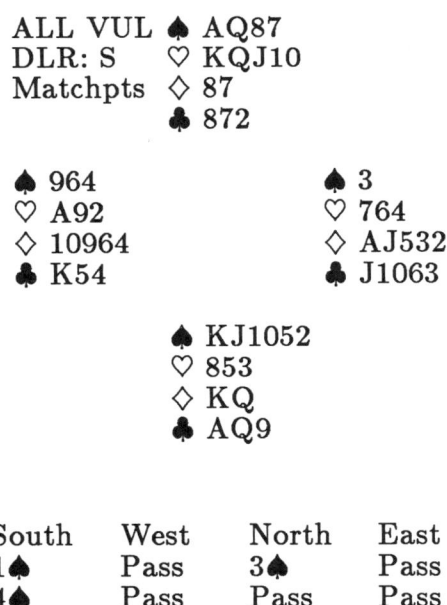

ALL VUL ♠ AQ87
DLR: S ♡ KQJ10
Matchpts ◇ 87
♣ 872

♠ 964   ♠ 3
♡ A92   ♡ 764
◇ 10964   ◇ AJ532
♣ K54   ♣ J1063

♠ KJ1052
♡ 853
◇ KQ
♣ AQ9

South	West	North	East
1♠	Pass	3♠	Pass
4♠	Pass	Pass	Pass

The opening lead against your 4♠ is the diamond

four, East winning and continuing the suit. At trick three you lead a spade to dummy, but instead of continuing spades, you immediately switch to the heart king following suit with the eight. It is technically best to pull trumps. Later hearts may be used for a club discard and the club finesse taken. Playing only one round of trumps risks a later heart ruff. But look at what may happen when West wins the heart ace at trick three. This may be the view in his mind's eye:

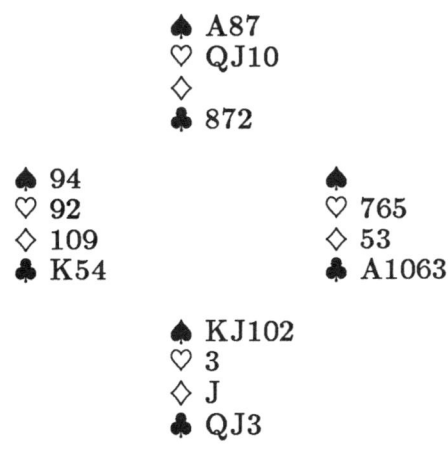

Sneaky player that you are known to be, you have convinced West that a signal from East will be revealing of club strength. Acting on his convictions, West smartly switches to clubs and you have eleven tricks.

Of course, you would have played the hand exactly this way had you held two losing clubs. These types of hands are extraordinarily interesting because they require a breadth of vision both on the part of the declarer and the defenders. The declarer must project other possible hands and how he would play them, and probable defenses; the defenders must be good enough to envision the holding declarer wishes to suggest. In a way, this means that such traps will only work when they are matched to the skill of the defenders. On rare occasions the defenders need to be world caliber.

We have seen that declarer will often want to leave trumps outstanding in order to avoid a discard which will help the defenders. More often, pulling trumps is essential to the play but the opponents hold a high one. In that case, it is important to lose the trick immediately, even if there is a better technical line. In the following hand, based on an idea of Kelsey's, South gives up the slight chance of bringing in the trump suit for no losers in order to avoid a defensive discard. Take the West seat first.

```
ALL VUL   ♠ A73
DLR: S    ♡ Q965
          ◇ KQ
          ♣ 10743

♠ QJ10
♡ J10
◇ J9432
♣ J86
```

South	West	North	East
1♠	Pass	2♣	4◇*
6♣	Pass	6♠	Pass
Pass	Pass		

*=very distributional diamond-heart two suiter

After a spirited auction, you try the jack of hearts as your opening lead. Play proceeds with the queen, king and ace. South continues with the two of spades at trick two. When you split your honors dummy ducks! How do you continue? It might seem that you have absolutely nothing to assist you here. Either a diamond or a heart might be right. The reason for your problem is that East was not able to give you the count in any suit. Presumably declarer has K-sixth of spades and has given up the possibility of finding spades 2-2. It is not absolutely certain whether this is the best plan, but in any case what do you return?

Did you continue hearts?

Then you were right.

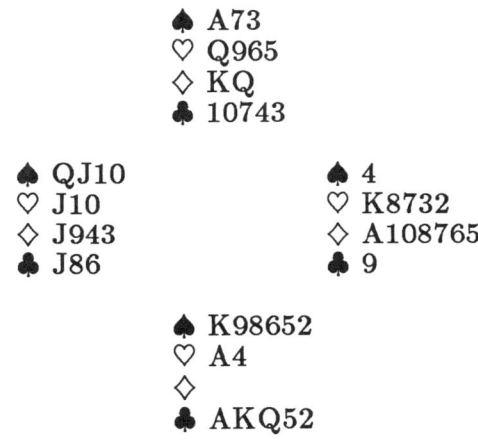

Obviously a diamond return provides South with a pitch. In fact, there was a clue here. If East had held six hearts, he would not have covered the queen. It would not help the defense any more to find declarer with singleton ace than it would to find him with ace-ten doubleton.

On other occasions, there may not even be a good technical line. Then the only hope for success lies with putting it to the defense at the earliest possible moment. Here is a hand from club play:

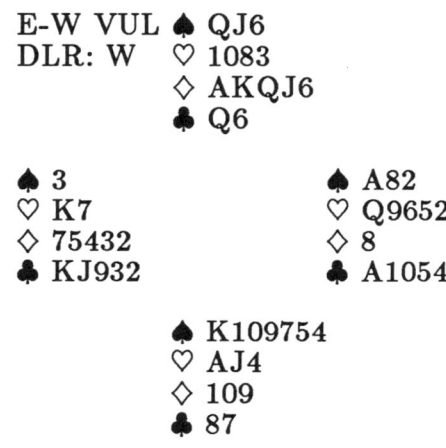

E-W VUL ♠ QJ6
DLR: W ♡ 1083
◇ AKQJ6
♣ Q6

♠ 3
♡ K7
◇ 75432
♣ KJ932

♠ A82
♡ Q9652
◇ 8
♣ A1054

♠ K109754
♡ AJ4
◇ 109
♣ 87

West	North	East	South
Pass	1◇	1♡	1♠
Pass	1NT*	Pass	2♣**
Pass	2♠	Pass	4♠
Pass	Pass	Pass	

*=15-17 balanced   **=artificial check-back

After the bidding shown, West began with the heart king. The fatal flaw in this contract is the lack of the spade ace. Without a doubt, first round controls of key suits are undervalued by Standard point count methods. Not only will games fail without them, many a 27-point slam succeeds because the first round controls belong to declarer. Seeing little chance of success for a hold-up, declarer won immediately and began trumps, low to the queen. And now disaster struck. Since the three of spades looked innocent enough, East barged ahead with the queen of hearts and a third one. Instead of down one, South had an overtrick.

In some ways, this hand might have belonged to the last chapter. There is an enormous sense of thrill that comes with giving partner a ruff. Here you are, forced to play in the opponents' ball park, by their rules, and you've turned the tables on them. Bridge disaster is the frequent consequence of hurried excitement. Certainly, East should have considered the possibility that the declarer began with six trumps. Since South needed at least five spades for his bidding it would not have hurt to cash the club ace first. West will encourage and the contract will gently go down.

Many times the most either side can hope for is to provide room for error to the other. South did that on this hand.

Sometimes declarer holds a side-suit so worthless and unprotected that he may feel there is no hope of avoiding losers there. If the defenders cards are arranged in tenaces, however, they may have great reluctance to strike out from that suit, even at the highest level. When this next hand was played in Biarritz in 1982, Jaime Diaz-Agero was lauded in the press for finding the winning defensive play, as West, while other defenders in his direction failed. It may be that even more credit should go to his partner.

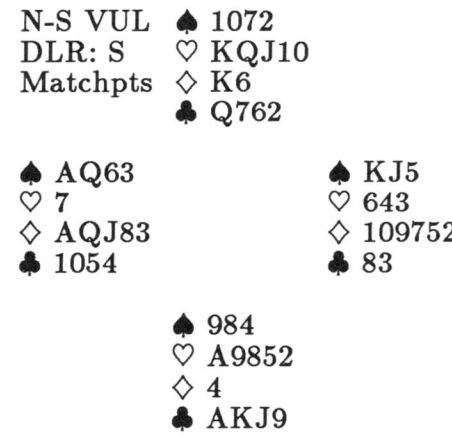

```
N-S VUL    ♠ 1072
DLR: S     ♡ KQJ10
Matchpts   ◇ K6
           ♣ Q762

♠ AQ63              ♠ KJ5
♡ 7                 ♡ 643
◇ AQJ83             ◇ 109752
♣ 1054              ♣ 83

           ♠ 984
           ♡ A9852
           ◇ 4
           ♣ AKJ9
```

In every case the contract was 4♡, played by South. Reluctant to attack from his tenaces, Diaz-Agero began with a trump. As one can see, there are four losers. Putting the defense to the brink immediately, South overtook the ten with his ace and returned the diamond. West won the ace and East made the excellent play of dropping the ten. After thinking for some time, West

60

returned a low spade.

It should be noted that the declarer gave it his best shot. He made the critical play early, before pulling trumps to allow a spade signal. And he entered the South hand in trumps rather that expose the club position.

Throughout this chapter, the emphasis has been on declarer play. There is one critically important set of hands which fall into the defenders' province. These are hands where discovery play will permit declarer to eventually take the correct position on a finesse.

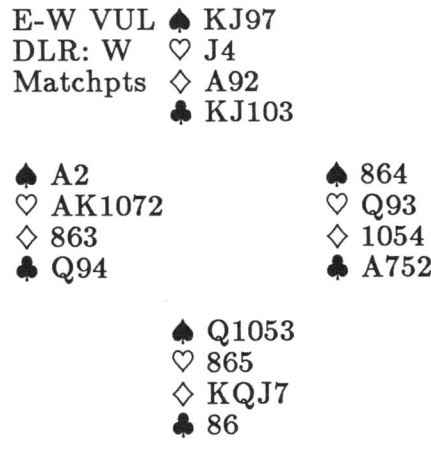

```
E-W VUL  ♠ KJ97
DLR: W   ♡ J4
Matchpts ♢ A92
         ♣ KJ103

♠ A2              ♠ 864
♡ AK1072          ♡ Q93
♢ 863             ♢ 1054
♣ Q94             ♣ A752

         ♠ Q1053
         ♡ 865
         ♢ KQJ7
         ♣ 86
```

West	North	East	South
1♡	DBL	2♡	2♠
Pass	Pass	Pass	

This is the kind of hand that gets played wrong every day in club games and no one notices. Typically,

West begins with three rounds of hearts, South ruffing. When West gets in with his ace of spades, he may switch to a club, but against a competent declarer it is too late. While an occasional East may venture a raise on four points, South is certain to disregard that slim possibility and place East with the ace of clubs. As the only chance to cause his opponent to err, West must switch to clubs at trick three.

Since the opening lead belongs to the defenders, they have the opportunity to force a guess the earliest. We'll conclude with a truly classic hand for the defense, starring Fred Karpin, but one still worth recalling and enjoying.

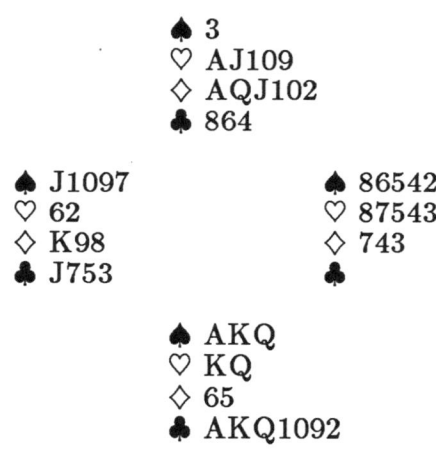

South played in 7NT, after advertising his powerful club suit and Karpin found the killing lead of the diamond nine. Any other lead will allow declarer the time he needs to discover the critical club distribution. The fortunate diamond position would be there to rescue him at the end. Of course, with no reason to risk his contract at trick one. South played the ace and had to fail.

Chapter 5
AUCTION ANTICS

Why do you bid what you do? Generally it is to construct a route to the appropriate final contract. However, if you think about it, the appropriateness of the final contract may well depend on the bids you made getting there. Consider this hand which came up a short time ago in our club game.

```
N-S VUL    ♠ AK4
DLR: N     ♡ 96
           ♢ 72
           ♣ AQ8643


           ♠ Q973
           ♡ AJ1073
           ♢ A4
           ♣ 52
```

Our auction proceeded: 1♣ − 1♡, 2♣ − 2♠, 3♣ − P. Making four. Although ten tricks were makable, I expected a good result. Moysian fits are notoriously difficult to get to. Frequently they also play for only 9 tricks when game is bid (which is not the best way to play matchpoints). On the other hand, the heart game, not terrible in the 5-2, would only be reached if we committed the hand to game, bidding 4♡ over 3♠. That would really work out badly if North were 1-3 in the reds instead.

Unfortunately, the scoring slip at the end of the night recorded 3NT played four of eight times, and defeated only once. Apparently the bidding had gone: 1♣ − 1♡, 2♣ − 2NT, 3NT − P, and the defense had led spades. Now, the fact is, I liked our bidding and play. But, the fact also was that we ended up with an average on the board.

All this is to show that overly constructive bidding pays a price. You avoid bad contracts at the expense of missing some really good ones because *hand killing* information has been given to the opponents. Clearly the defense would have started diamonds against $3NT$ at our table.

Now there are two ways to use bidding to make life difficult for your opponents. One is to avoid declaring your assets while heading to the most likely final contract. This is the route employed by the no-trump bidders, above. The other is to make "incorrect" bids when you think the opponents are listening. Of course, the second are much more *exciting*, but also more dangerous. As a rule, this second kind of bidding occurs more frequently on defense:

```
NONE V.    ♠ QJ64
DLR: W     ♡ 95
           ♢ K2
           ♣ A10864

♠ A975              ♠ K832
♡ QJ                ♡ K832
♢ AQ975             ♢ J6
♣ K9                ♣ Q53

           ♠ 10
           ♡ A10764
           ♢ 10843
           ♣ J72
```

West	North	East	South
1NT	Pass	2♣	Pass
2♠	Pass	3♠	Pass
4♠	Pass	Pass	DBL
Pass	Pass	Pass	

East-West reluctantly agree on 4♠ after employing Stayman, and, against unsuspecting declarers, a double by South is definitely a consideration. There are three things going for it. First, North is likely to hold a fair 10 count behind the no-trumper, and, second, the trumps are splitting badly.

However, a third consequence of the double is that declarer may play you for trump tricks. After the ♡9 lead is won in the South hand and a diamond is returned to the king, North can exit with a red suit card, either immediately, or after cashing the ♣A. At this point, West has several ways to hold the damage to one down. When he plays the ♠K from the board, though, (playing

North for stiff Q, J, or 10) the result is +300 to the defense.

Not being faint-hearted you pick up, not-vulnerable, the following hand:

♠ 94
♡ J9
♢ AK109632
♣ QJ

1♠	1NT*
2♡	3NT

*=forcing

There are really three ways to bid this hand. If you decide to play in game, you can show your diamond suit or not. If you do show your suit, you will be embarrassed if this pinpoints a lead for the opponents. If you do not force to game with this hand, then you will have to accept a plus score at 3♢ when your partner passes out the likely misfit. Then, if the game is always making you will undoubtedly get a poor result. At the table, West led a heart. This was not a rousing success, since only a black suit lead would have worked.

```
            ♠ AJ752
            ♡ AKQ10
            ◇ 5
            ♣ 973

♠ Q1086              ♠ K3
♡ 8432               ♡ 765
◇ Q4                 ◇ J87
♣ K105               ♣ A8642

            ♠ 94
            ♡ J9
            ◇ AK109632
            ♣ QJ
```

Declarer was careful to win the heart in dummy, high, preserving the jack as an entry, and take a first round finesse of the ◇10.

Try a lead problem. What would you lead from this collection?

♠ 642
♡ J9753
♢ K42
♣ 86

East	South	West	North
1♠	Pass	3♠	Pass
4♣	Pass	4NT	Pass
5♢	DBL	6♠	Pass
Pass	Pass		

Before you lead, you had better realize that you are North; your partner is on lead! He has made a **Lead-Out-of-Turn-Directing** double. Here is a typical hand.

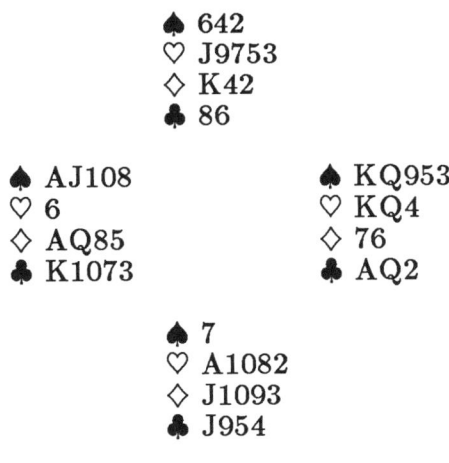

```
                ♠ 642
                ♡ J9753
                ♢ K42
                ♣ 86
♠ AJ108                    ♠ KQ953
♡ 6                        ♡ KQ4
♢ AQ85                     ♢ 76
♣ K1073                    ♣ AQ2
                ♠ 7
                ♡ A1082
                ♢ J1093
                ♣ J954
```

As it happens, East can make his slam, with a third round club finesse, but he is likely to fail.

Occasionally, the bidding will be almost the same, and the result quite different.

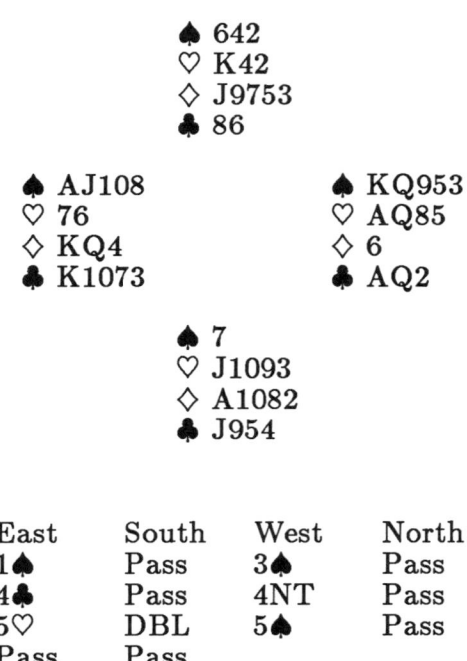

East	South	West	North
1♠	Pass	3♠	Pass
4♣	Pass	4NT	Pass
5♡	DBL	5♠	Pass
Pass	Pass		

The requirements for a lead-out-of-turn-directing double are not fixed in stone, but they tend to be a fair idea that your side has at least one trick, and a conviction that the opponents may mis-evaluate their assets in another suit.

Another way that spurious doubling can achieve unexpected results is the well-known "striped-tail" ape
double.

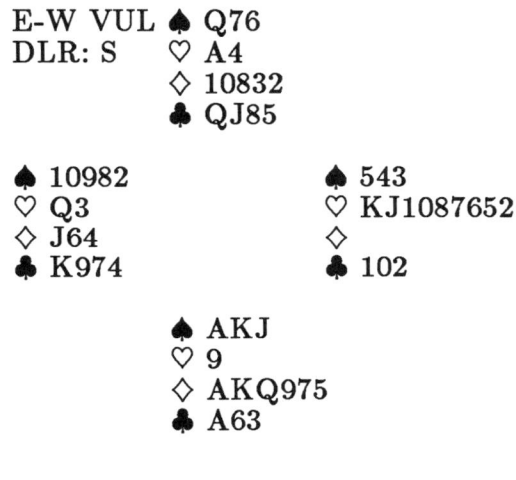

```
E-W VUL    ♠ Q76
DLR: S     ♡ A4
           ♢ 10832
           ♣ QJ85

♠ 10982              ♠ 543
♡ Q3                 ♡ KJ1087652
♢ J64                ♢
♣ K974               ♣ 102

           ♠ AKJ
           ♡ 9
           ♢ AKQ975
           ♣ A63
```

South	West	North	East
2♣	Pass	2NT	Pass!!
3♢	Pass	4♢	Pass
4NT	Pass	5♢	DBL!
Pass???	Pass	Pass	

Yes, there are Souths who forget to redouble. As the
cards lie, declarer makes 12 tricks for +650, well below
the +920 available for the diamond slam. But there is
a second way that East-West can succeed. If South had
redoubled, then East can turn his tail and run to 5♡.
Occasionally this will get doubled. As a final contract,
it is not as profitable as 5♢×, but only yields +800 to
the opponents.

Yet a third way to use doubling anti-constructively is to offer the opponents a chance to play a redoubled contract at the 5-level rather than slam at the 6- or 7-level. In this venture, as with the striped- tail ape double, you are aided often by two facts, the scoring structure and the opponents' frequent misunderstanding of it. The following hand made up a large portion of the +120 IMPs gained in the Salt Lake City National IMP-pairs. My partner, Nick Hartung, who encouraged this disaster, is normally a very conservative and steady player – which just shows that no massive ego is needed to harass your opponents into the pit – an innocent little double may suffice.

```
N-S VUL    ♠ KQJ109
DLR: S     ♡ J
           ◇ Q1084
           ♣ Q94

♠ 7632              ♠ 854
♡ Q9763             ♡ AK842
◇ K965              ◇ 7
♣                   ♣ 8762

           ♠ A
           ♡ 105
           ◇ AJ32
           ♣ AKJ1053
```

South	West	North	East
1♣	Pass	1♠	Pass
3♣	Pass	4♣	Pass
4◇	Pass	4NT	Pass
5◇*	DBL	RDBL!!	Pass
Pass???	Pass		

*=4 key-cards for clubs

A little consultation with the scoring sheet will convince anyone of the futility of this venture. Making 6♣ would have won our opponents +1370 points. Since the datum turned out to be about +1100, this would have ensured a fine IMP result of +7. Five diamonds redoubled making six returns +1400, for a *large* improvement of 0 IMP.

However, against a certain bad split in the trump suit, perhaps North-South should have revised their estimate down to making just 11 tricks in diamonds. For this effort, they enjoy a +1000 bonus. Unfortunately, this translates into a three IMP loss. To make a long story short, Nick, bless his soul, managed to find a heart lead. The heart continuation tapped dummy and gave declarer a problem which he did not solve. When the smoke cleared, North-South were down one. The +400 points for the set, plus +1100 for the datum gave us the good result instead (17 IMPs!).

Against highly aggressive bidders, everyone vulnerable, you hear this uncontested auction:

1♠	4♢*
4♠	5♢*
5♡	6♠
Pass	

The diamond bids show initially a singleton, but then first-round control. What do you lead from...

♠ 765
♡ AJ1042
♢ A984
♣ 6   ?

Would you change your lead if the auction had proceeded differently?

1♠	5NT*
7♠	Pass

*=Grand Slam Force

If you chose a club or heart, you might be chagrined to see dummy. These were the hands:

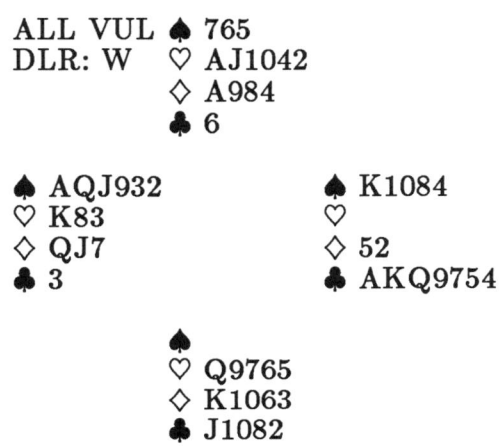

```
ALL VUL   ♠ 765
DLR: W    ♡ AJ1042
          ◇ A984
          ♣ 6

♠ AQJ932          ♠ K1084
♡ K83             ♡
◇ QJ7             ◇ 52
♣ 3               ♣ AKQ9754

          ♠
          ♡ Q9765
          ◇ K1063
          ♣ J1082
```

In a Houston sectional, 1961, you sit down East against Ozzie Jacoby on your left. North is dealer and the bidding proceeds:

North	South
1♡	2◇
2♡	3NT
Pass	

Your partner leads the ♠4 and you see:

```
♠ K63
♡ AK9642
◇ K86
♣ 9
```

```
          ♠ A5
          ♡ 3
          ◇ J9752
          ♣ J8643
```

Jacoby plays the king off dummy and wins the spade return with the queen in the closed hand. He continues with the ♡Q from hand, and two more rounds of hearts. On the last heart, Jacoby throws a small diamond from his own hand; meanwhile you have discarded the fifth card from each of your two minor suits. At trick six, a low spade is called from the dummy. Your play.

The actual defender discarded another club. Jacoby then remarked calmly, "Here come the British!" These were the hands:

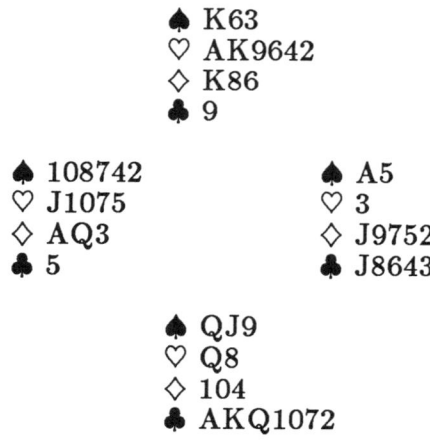

```
              ♠ K63
              ♡ AK9642
              ◇ K86
              ♣ 9

♠ 108742              ♠ A5
♡ J1075               ♡ 3
◇ AQ3                 ◇ J9752
♣ 5                   ♣ J8643

              ♠ QJ9
              ♡ Q8
              ◇ 104
              ♣ AKQ1072
```

False cue-bids are a well-known ploy but they can be very effective if used infrequently. Still, they mislead partner and not always the opponents, so, should you choose to employ them, beware.

If you ever have the chance to play a match against Alan Sontag, it will be your distinct pleasure. Sontag is a fantastic player, a real thrill to watch in action, and the odds are, he'll make short work of you and your team-mates. Bridge being what it is, though, on a good day you might just win — — unless you try to keep pace with him. You see, almost no one plays as *f-a-s-t ! !* and as well as Sontag, at least in that combination. If Pete Carrill and the Princeton University basketball team have taught us anything, it's that the only possibility the little guys have of beating the big guys is to set the pace of play. Once you adopt your opponents' tempo, you are at a distinct disadvantage.

Unless you are a very quick thinker, it is unlikely that fast play will help you gain an advantage over your adversaries, and deliberately varying your routine to pressure your opponents borders on the unethical. It is expected that you will make all your plays at a reasonably constant pace. The other way to gain an advantage will certainly make you any number of enemies. That is to employ the Sominex coup, take so long to play that everyone falls asleep by the time their turns come around. (Sominex is an over-the-counter sleep medication.)

On the other hand, there are certain auctions that generate a tempo of their own and which can lull the other pair to destruction. Especially important is the 'doubling tempo'. Once the opponents smell blood, they will find it hard to let go. Since this book is dedicated to Mel Lawhorn, it is only right to enjoy a classic hand he played on the way to winning an ABA National Pairs Championship. This hand comes by way of an immensely enjoyable, but sadly unpublished book by

Jim Garcia, *A Nostalgic Reminiscence in the American Bridge Association.*

Playing two-way no-trumps, 11-14 HCP non-vulnerable, the following auction took place:

North	East	South	West
1NT	DBL	2♣	DBL
Pass	Pass	2♢	DBL
Pass	Pass	2♡	DBL
Pass	Pass	2♠	DBL
Pass	Pass	Pass	

These were the four hands:

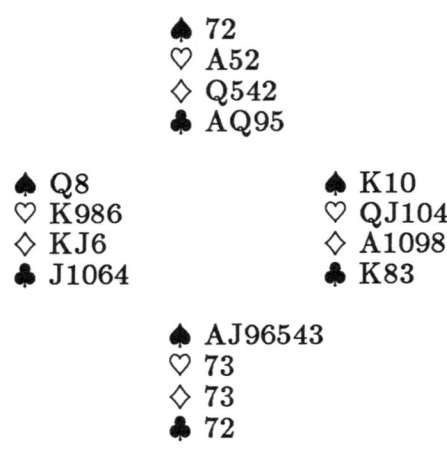

```
              ♠ 72
              ♡ A52
              ♢ Q542
              ♣ AQ95

♠ Q8                      ♠ K10
♡ K986                    ♡ QJ104
♢ KJ6                     ♢ A1098
♣ J1064                   ♣ K83

              ♠ AJ96543
              ♡ 73
              ♢ 73
              ♣ 72
```

Lawhorn went on to make three.

Chapter 6
INVITATION TO ANNIHILATION

In the movies, the bad guys are often disposed of by engineered collisions. The good guy, some way or another, manages to invite or coerce the meetings of heads, two at a time, and the villains lie crumpled on the floor, with headaches.

The same can be attempted at the bridge table, of course. There what declarer does is induce the collision of top honors. In order to achieve this result, which, by the way, causes some of the choicest arguments and recriminations in bridgedom, it is necessary to hide crucial details about length and strength from the defense.

Take a look at these three combinations:

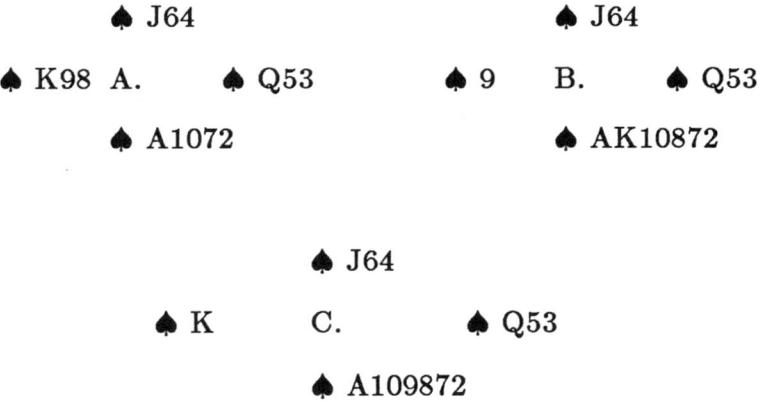

When declarer calls for the ♠J from dummy, East has a problem. In A, he must cover to limit North-South to one trick. In B, if he does not cover, he will very often gain a trick, declarer playing for an even split. Finally, in C, covering elicits squeals of merriment from all impartial observers and you finally learn that all those illiterates in your group actually do know the definition of regicide.

Now the other guys' books will tell you all about when to cover, and when not to. But this is a compendium on creating problems for the opponents, so we won't worry about whether they'd get it right, just about how to give them the chance to blow it.

As we've seen before, errors are most prone to happen when little information is known about the hand. A common situation where this occurs is in no-trump auctions where you have violated all sense of decency and opened with a five-card major.

After an auction that runs, 1 *NT* - 2♣ - 2♠ - 4♠, lefty tables the ♡*Q* and this is what you get:

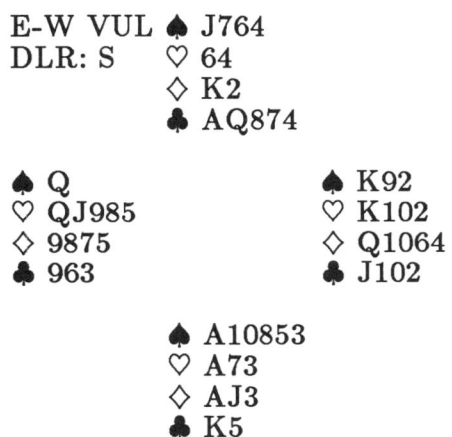

E-W VUL ♠ J764
DLR: S ♡ 64
◇ K2
♣ AQ874

♠ Q
♡ QJ985
◇ 9875
♣ 963

♠ K92
♡ K102
◇ Q1064
♣ J102

♠ A10853
♡ A73
◇ AJ3
♣ K5

Playing matchpoints, you win the first heart, enter dummy with a diamond and call for the ♠*J*. East, who has been reading someone else's article pictures the following:

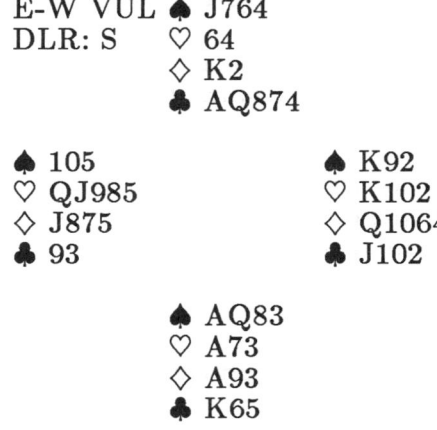

E-W VUL ♠ J764
DLR: S ♡ 64
        ◇ K2
        ♣ AQ874

♠ 105   ♠ K92
♡ QJ985   ♡ K102
◇ J875   ◇ Q1064
♣ 93   ♣ J102

        ♠ AQ83
        ♡ A73
        ◇ A93
        ♣ K65

He, therefore, swings high, neatly decapitating his partner's queen. When the smoke clears, thanks to a 3-3 club division and the marked trump finesse, you have all 13 tricks. "Next hand please, gentlemen; post-mortems later."

Try a declarer problem.

```
N-S VUL    ♠ 52
DLR: N     ♡ K3
           ◇ AKJ4
           ♣ Q7642

           ♠ AK3
           ♡ Q74
           ◇ 109832
           ♣ J3
```

North	East	South	West
1◇	DBL	RDBL	1♠
2♣	Pass	2NT	Pass
3NT	Pass	Pass	Pass

The opening lead is the spade jack to your ace. Relying on East's take out double you try a diamond finesse which holds, all following. On the subsequent ace and king of diamonds, East discards two small clubs. How should you continue?

At the table, declarer, Zia Mahmood, reasoned as follows. East must have a five card club suit to account for the discards, but from *AK*-fifth he might rather have parted with hearts. So Zia played the ♣*Q*, and East covered. Kaboom!

N-S VUL   ♠ 52
DLR: N   ♡ K3
            ◇ AKJ4
            ♣ Q7642

♠ J10974	♠ Q86
♡ 10862	♡ AJ95
◇ Q75	◇ 6
♣ A	♣ K10985

            ♠ AK3
            ♡ Q74
            ◇ 109832
            ♣ J3

It may seem that the rules of bridge prohibit a defender from capturing his own high cards with other honors in his hand. This is a mere technicality which can be overcome by creative card play.

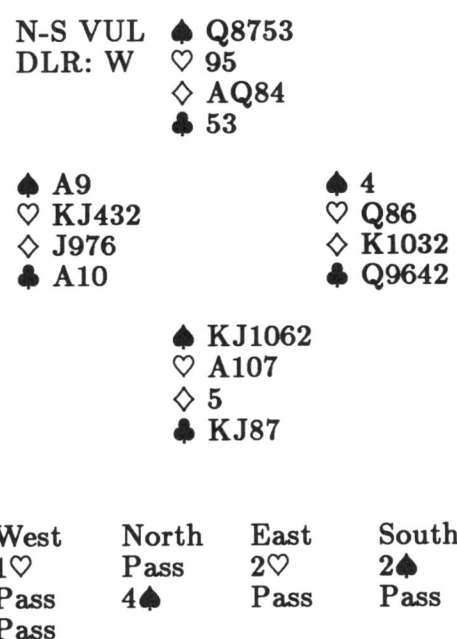

N-S VUL ♠ Q8753
DLR: W ♡ 95
◇ AQ84
♣ 53

♠ A9   ♠ 4
♡ KJ432   ♡ Q86
◇ J976   ◇ K1032
♣ A10   ♣ Q9642

♠ KJ1062
♡ A107
◇ 5
♣ KJ87

West	North	East	South
1♡	Pass	2♡	2♠
Pass	4♠	Pass	Pass
Pass			

In this example, which was suggested by a Mike Lawrence theme, South captures the heart queen at trick one and returns a heart. Suppose that West wins and plays two rounds of trumps. Now declarer wins, ruffs a heart in dummy, and continues with the ace and queen of diamonds. Should East play high, he will not only have covered dummy's queen, but decapitated his own. With the jack of diamonds and club queen alone to be accounted for, West surely must hold the ace of clubs for his opening bid. Declarer will have no choice but to play East for the queen. If, instead, East plays low confidently at the critical moment, certain that South intends to ruff, declarer is likely to guess wrong later.

Related Ideas and Examples

There is a converse to the idea discussed in this section. Occasionally, it will clearly seem wrong to cover an honor with an honor. Usually this involves a situation in which ducking will ultimately promote one's own high card. For instance:

♠ K863

♠ Q led by declarer ♠ A2

In a no-trump contract, covering with the king in this situation would seem to be wrong. Declarer can come to two spade tricks but, subsequently, the ♠*K* will be high. Because this situation is *so* obvious, it can be employed to declarer's benefit. Consider this hand, played by Mark Lair in the 1986 Atlanta Reisinger:

E-W VUL ♠ K1097
DLR: E   ♡ A2
        ♢ K1054
        ♣ Q106

♠ 85432   ♠ Q
♡ K863   ♡ J74
♢ 2   ♢ AQ763
♣ 873   ♣ J542

         ♠ AJ6
         ♡ Q1095
         ♢ J98
         ♣ AK9

After a straightforward 1*NT* − 3*NT*, Lair, South, got the lead of the ♣8. He won in hand and ran the ◇*J* to East's queen. After winning the club return again in hand. He continued diamonds, ducked by East. Then, before knocking out the ◇*A*, Lair passed the ♡*Q*. When West *intelligently* played low, declarer reverted to diamonds, making 11 tricks.

In some no-trump contracts, declarer has a difficult time finding entries to a long suit in dummy. This problem occurs so often that most defenders are aware of the need to hold up winners to prevent entries. As a result, when a lack of entries is the problem one may often generate a needed extra trick by advancing unsupported honors.

```
N-S VUL   ♠ 653
DLR: S    ♡ 432
          ◇ 107
          ♣ J9642

♠ Q9742              ♠ J108
♡ 9765               ♡ A8
◇ 42                 ◇ J9853
♣ Q10                ♣ A73

          ♠ AK
          ♡ KQJ10
          ◇ AKQ6
          ♣ K85
```

South	West	North	East
2♣	Pass	2◇	Pass
3NT	Pass	Pass	Pass

After the exuberance accompanying receipt of a 25 point hand wore off, South suddenly noticed that the lead of the spade four was a killer. He was destined to lose three spade tricks and at least two aces. However, the anemic dummy still posed a threat of establishable clubs. Without hesitation, South won the first trick with the ace (thereby clumsily announcing that he also had the king), and tabled the king of clubs. East could not be certain what was going on, but the ten from partner seemed like the beginning of an echo from two. Having stolen a club trick, South switched to the heart suit, making his contract.

In suit contracts, the quick taking of winners is important for the defense since ruffs may come into play. In no-trump contracts where length winners are more often critical, bold moves such as this are more likely to succeed. We saw a similar situation arise in Chapter 2.

The British authors often rebuke those who fly with aces in second position by saying they fear "the rats would get at them." That fear is increased with lower valued honors. Consider each of these matrices:

In both cases, South is double-dummy destined to lose two tricks in the play of the suit. However, if he begins by leading low toward the J-third, a panicky West can contract his side's winners to one by rising with the queen.

Even when the jack is not in dummy, disaster can strike when a duck would leave the honor vulnerable:

Again, South is destined to lose two tricks. If he leads low from hand, West may play the queen realizing that it will be vulnerable on the next round. If he does, South's losers in the suit reduce to one.

One advantage which the experienced player often holds against a weaker one might well be called the "No finesse through me!" syndrome. There is a tendency for weaker players to assume that better players can see through the backs of the cards. As a result, tricks are often compacted by the play of intermediate honors as a way of warding off "winning" finesses. Consider the following suit combination:

♡ AJ832

♡ K1097　G.　　　♡ Q

♡ 654

Ignoring the possibility of a 5-0 split in the heart suit, the technical odds of playing the ace first, or low to the eight, are equal when trying to hold heart losers to two. Against weak opponents, it is a good idea to lead low from the South hand. Frequently, a defender in the West seat will anticipate a finesse of the eight and insert the nine spot. Now playing the ace holds your heart losers to one.

The following hand practically played itself at a Sectional Open Pairs:

```
N-S VUL    ♠ A82
DLR: S     ♡ A642
           ◇ 97
           ♣ Q832

♠ KQ107              ♠ 9
♡ 853                ♡ J109
◇ 1052               ◇ AQJ843
♣ A106               ♣ 974

           ♠ J6543
           ♡ KQ7
           ◇ K6
           ♣ KJ5
```

South	West	North	East
1♠	Pass	1NT*	3◇
Pass	Pass	3♠**	Pass
Pass	Pass		

*=one-round force
**=limit raise with 3 trump

The opening lead was the diamond two, and East won and returned a diamond. On the lead of a small spade at trick three, West inserted the *ten*. Dummy's ace won this trick and a club was played to the jack and ace. West woke up and tapped declarer with a third diamond, but South shed a heart from dummy, ruffed in his hand, and led another spade toward dummy. This was the position when West won the king:

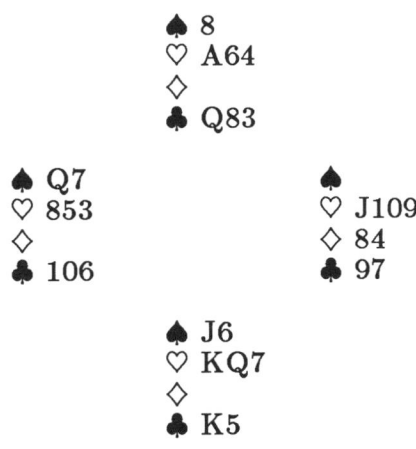

```
              ♠ 8
              ♡ A64
              ◇
              ♣ Q83
  ♠ Q7                    ♠
  ♡ 853                   ♡ J109
  ◇                       ◇ 84
  ♣ 106                   ♣ 97
              ♠ J6
              ♡ KQ7
              ◇
              ♣ K5
```

Regardless of the return, South would win, play a small trump from hand, win the next return, and pull trump and claim. Needless to say, East and West had much to discuss afterwards. Although, here, South naturally found himself in the closed hand at trick two, it will often be necessary to delay playing the critical suit until the lead can be made through the defender who holds length in that suit.

Especially in a weak field, honors stand out more than spot cards, simply because they are more memorable. If you boldly attack a suit with an honor card, you can sometimes direct the defense away from a profitable approach to one beneficial to the declarer. In this hand from a club matchpoint game, South both encouraged the right defender to win a trick, and induced a fatal switch.

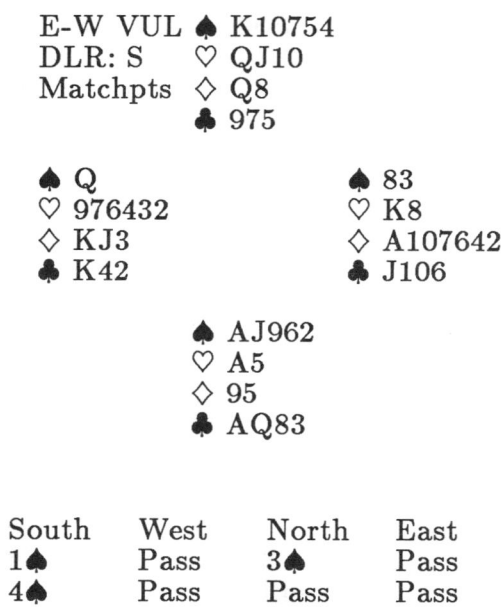

```
E-W VUL  ♠ K10754
DLR: S   ♡ QJ10
Matchpts ♢ Q8
         ♣ 975

♠ Q                      ♠ 83
♡ 976432                 ♡ K8
♢ KJ3                    ♢ A107642
♣ K42                    ♣ J106

         ♠ AJ962
         ♡ A5
         ♢ 95
         ♣ AQ83
```

South	West	North	East
1♠	Pass	3♠	Pass
4♠	Pass	Pass	Pass

After a borderline limit raise from North, declarer played in the spade game. The opening lead was the heart four to the queen, king and ace. Declarer played two rounds of spades, West pitching another small heart, and then played two rounds of hearts on which he discarded the diamond five and East the diamond seven.

At this point, the following cards remained:

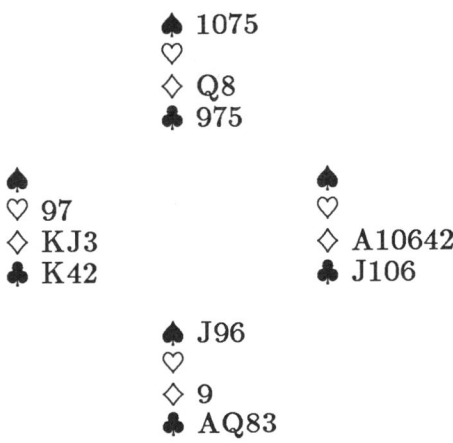

♠ 1075
♡
♦ Q8
♣ 975

♠
♡ 97
♦ KJ3
♣ K42

♠
♡
♦ A10642
♣ J106

♠ J96
♡
♦ 9
♣ AQ83

The trick at this point is to play the club suit for only one loser. As usual, it is much better to let the opponents attack the critical suit for you. Of course, there is clearly no way to guarantee any of this, but since West is unlikely to wish to attack clubs, the proper approach stands out. Wishing to put East on lead, and at the same time discourage a diamond continuation, declarer led the queen of diamonds from dummy. East pounced on this with the ace and promptly led the jack of clubs to the queen and ace. Although, West switched back to diamonds it was already to late to undo the damage. Declarer ruffed in hand, entered dummy and successfully finessed against East to make eleven tricks. This, of course, was tied for top board.

Chapter 7
LESSER REPTILIA

Some errors can only be avoided by a strong understanding of the game. For example, the Crocodile Coup is an advanced play that only the most jaded expert would not find thrilling to pull off. For those readers not familiar with this species of bridge animal, consider the following illustrative matrix:

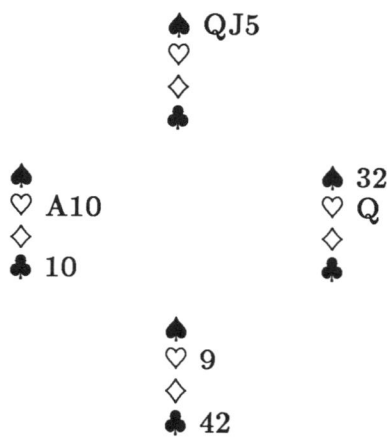

At no-trump, with South on lead, it is easy to see, double-dummy, that East-West can take all the remaining tricks. However, when declarer leads the ♡9, West must be careful to rise with the ace, thus *swallowing* East's queen. Otherwise, the last two tricks will elude the defenders.

While the Crocodile Coup usually makes its appearance near the very end of a hand, and generally involves honor cards, its sibling (say the *Gecko Coup*) occurs in the middle of the hand when it is imperative that one

opponent or the other be kept off lead. It is frequently the case that a small card can be ducked to a player who must do something damaging to his side. Since the Gecko is a sleepy lizard, it is not always prepared to flick out a high card to snag a low flying intruder. Further assistance comes from a very human attribute; the natural inclination to win a trick as cheaply as possible.

The following hand comes from Cohn and Fink's excellent and challenging book, *Power Defensive Carding*.

```
NONE V.   ♠ K10762
DLR: N    ♡ Q
          ♢ AQ104
          ♣ AK5

          ♠ J
          ♡ 97654
          ♢ K6
          ♣ QJ742
```

North	East	South	West
1♠	Pass	1NT	Pass
3♢	Pass	3NT	Pass
Pass	Pass		

Suppose you sit down in the South seat and declare 3*NT* after an uncontested auction. Your opponents are the club champ (East) and a fair but not spectacular West. The opening lead is the ♡3 (fourth best), and righty does an amazing thing. He wins the king and switches to the three of clubs. What is going on here?

Unless West has made a bizarre lead from AJ10-sixth, East is guaranteed to hold at least two hearts. If three, he would certainly continue the suit. For all East knows, his side has four or five ready heart tricks. On the other hand, West has not led an intermediate heart honor, so he cannot hold the AJ10. The conclusion is inescapable, East must have the KJ- or K10- tight in hearts. Why has he not continued hearts? It must be that he wants West to *overtake* the heart later on. It will certainly not be clear to West that he must overtake his partner's ♡J or ♡10 at trick two. So East has retained this winning exit card for use after gaining the lead later on.

You may not see all this immediately, but you play off two high clubs in dummy and RHO discards a spade. Now it should be clear. West began with five hearts and four clubs. It is likely that East holds both diamond length and spade length so running off diamonds or taking either finesse is unlikely to work. It's time to sneak by the gecko.

You lead a diamond to the king and place the ♡7 on the table. If lefty is a sleepy lizard, he will extend an eight, and the defense is finished. East may wriggle about in his chair but soon he will give you a ninth trick in spades or diamonds.

These are the hands.

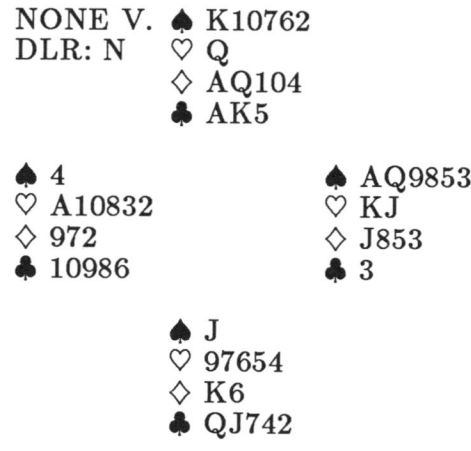

NONE V. ♠ K10762
DLR: N   ♡ Q
         ◇ AQ104
         ♣ AK5

♠ 4   ♠ AQ9853
♡ A10832   ♡ KJ
◇ 972   ◇ J853
♣ 10986   ♣ 3

         ♠ J
         ♡ 97654
         ◇ K6
         ♣ QJ742

Another time to catch the gecko asleep is when it looks like you are leading to a winner in dummy.

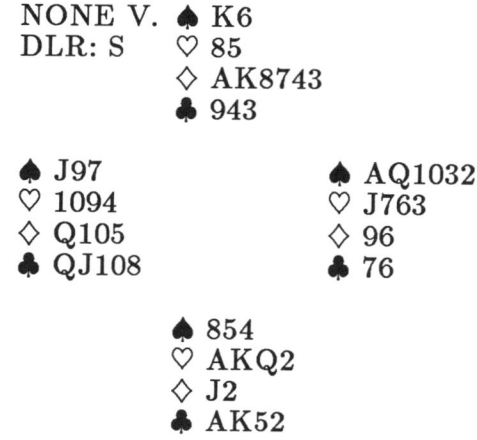

NONE V. ♠ K6
DLR: S   ♡ 85
         ◇ AK8743
         ♣ 943

♠ J97   ♠ AQ1032
♡ 1094   ♡ J763
◇ Q105   ◇ 96
♣ QJ108   ♣ 76

         ♠ 854
         ♡ AKQ2
         ◇ J2
         ♣ AK52

After $1NT$ - $3NT$, West, for better or worse, begins with the ♣Q. At trick two you begin diamonds with the two knowing that you need to duck a round. A lazy defender may play low allowing you to keep the danger hand off-lead. Of course, if the cards were slightly different:

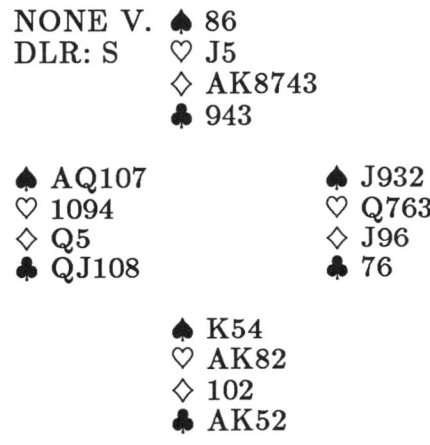

NONE V. ♠ 86
DLR: S ♡ J5
        ◇ AK8743
        ♣ 943

♠ AQ107   ♠ J932
♡ 1094   ♡ Q763
◇ Q5   ◇ J96
♣ QJ108   ♣ 76

        ♠ K54
        ♡ AK82
        ◇ 102
        ♣ AK52

you would play the ◇10 to encourage West to cover.

On some occasions, the suit you are leading is one in which dummy is void. Instead of ruffing, however, you plan a loser-on-loser play instead. If the geckos are sleeping you will make hands such as the following:

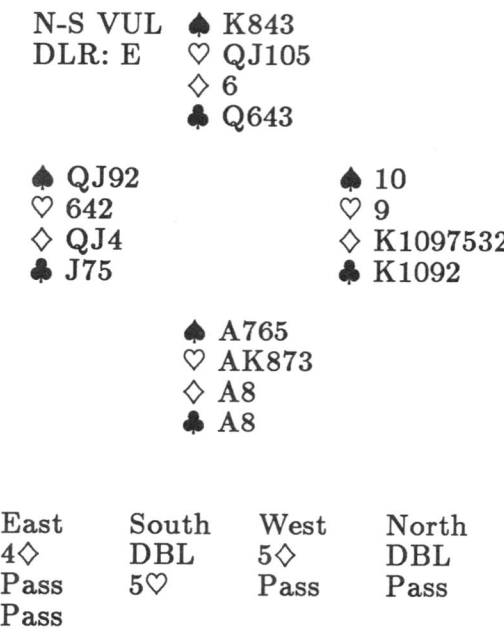

	♠ K843
N-S VUL	♡ QJ105
DLR: E	◇ 6
	♣ Q643

♠ QJ92		♠ 10
♡ 642		♡ 9
◇ QJ4		◇ K1097532
♣ J75		♣ K1092

	♠ A765
	♡ AK873
	◇ A8
	♣ A8

East	South	West	North
4◇	DBL	5◇	DBL
Pass	5♡	Pass	Pass
Pass			

After a highly competitive auction, the vulnerability convinced South to forego the +300 penalty for defending. West began with a high diamond to South's ace. The declarer led a spade to the king, cashed the queen and jack of hearts, and continued with a spade to the ace. For his two discards East found small diamonds. This was not particularly convincing, the diamond king would perhaps have woken the sleepy West. In any event, at trick five, declarer offered his Left Hand

Friend the eight of diamonds, but he declined it playing the lowly four instead. Dummy expelled a spade and declarer could not be prevented from making 11 tricks. In practice, East continued with another diamond giving declarer a ruff and sluff for the eleventh trick.

Curiously, the alternative line of the strip and endplay only works if another gecko coup succeeds. South proceeds as before but if West is awake enough to find the high diamond at trick six, declarer ruffs his losing diamond. Now after ace and a club, West must rise with the jack forcing dummy to cover. If instead he lazily contributes the seven, dummy ducks and East gets endplayed a different way. Now declarer loses a club and one spade rather than a diamond and another. Of course there is no guess on the club play. If lefty had the king of clubs, he would rise and cash out in spades when declarer leads toward the queen.

Chapter 8
TEMPO TELLS/censored!!!

In gambling, a *tell* is some inadvertent habit or action that gives away a player's holding. In the game of bridge, there are essentially two types of tells. These might be referred to as problem/no problem tells, and unethical-problem tells. As a matter of education, it is important to see how one might take advantage of unethical behavior on the part of the opponents, but the subject has an unsavory taste to it. A little preface concerning ethics is important.

Ideally, one must make all plays at the same tempo. But this is easier said than done. Certainly, problems arise in the play of the hand, especially on defense. For this reason, many players take time early in the play to project out possible problems to occur later on. In this way, when the problem situation arises, the defender can follow to the critical trick in tempo.

Even so, and especially with inexperienced players, there will be times when revealing hesitations are inevitable. While this gives away the position of key cards, it is a fact of bridge. This is a problem tell:

♡ KQ103

♡ A7

When declarer (W) leads a heart to dummy's queen in a 3NT contract, an inexperienced defender may hesitate. Even if he then ducks the trick, declarer is certain to finesse for a missing jack at the next go. While this

is unfortunate for the defender it is certainly not unethical. With greater experience he will learn to play
low smoothly. On the other hand, suppose these are the
suits:

♡ KQ103

♡ J7

Now a hesitation by South is completely unethical.
Behavior such as that would produce immediate and
justified ill-will. The successful and extremely ethical
American star, David Treadwell, once sat on defense
with the crucial suit sitting thus:

♣ KJ63

♣ Q105   ♣ A972

♣ 84

When a club was led from the South hand, West
hesitated, then played low. Before declarer called from
dummy, Treadwell immediately put his ace on the table.

Another unfortunate, but completely ethical tell occurs when fourth hand cannot see that there is a guess on the hand and detaches a card prematurely.

$$\spadesuit \text{ Q72}$$

$$\spadesuit \text{ A1098} \qquad \spadesuit \text{ KJ643}$$

$$\spadesuit \text{ 5}$$

In third seat you open the West hand with 1♠. Although your style is 5-card majors, you and your partner are more flexible in third and fourth positions. Your partner, with an 11 count and KJ-fifth in trump support bids game.

Well, the crucial moment comes when you lead ♠A and continue with a low one. But wait, RHO has already detached a card from his hand. You can almost take this one to the bank. He is not holding the queen, but rather a useless discard. This is the no-problem tell.

For an aspiring player, the lesson to be learned from all this is that acquiring a steady tempo is very important. On the other hand, none of these ethical tells can be reliably elicited from the opponents by declarer play. On the other hand, unethical tells can sometimes be summoned. When an opponent unethically pauses to gain an advantage, he deserves all the zeroes his play derives; and you will often gain. This next hand came from a New Jersey regional.

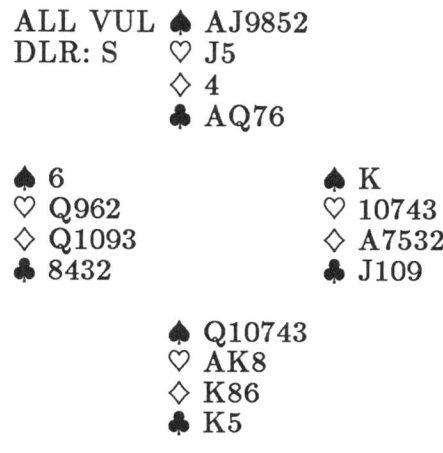

```
ALL VUL  ♠ AJ9852
DLR: S   ♡ J5
         ◇ 4
         ♣ AQ76

♠ 6                      ♠ K
♡ Q962                   ♡ 10743
◇ Q1093                  ◇ A7532
♣ 8432                   ♣ J109

         ♠ Q10743
         ♡ AK8
         ◇ K86
         ♣ K5
```

You declare 6♠ after opening the South hand 1♠, and the defense begins with two rounds of diamonds, you ruffing in dummy. Now, the odds favor playing for a drop in spades by the thinnest of margins, roughly 52% − 48%, but in the Open Pairs that just means you are tossing dice for a good score or a bad score. Against good defenders, you should just play the ace and hope that the king will drop, but you can give yourself a better chance against some others by delaying.

At the table, the play went ♣*A*, then club to the king. By now four tricks had been played. When the ♠*Q* was led, West *hitched*, then played low. The absence of a no-problem tell from East was inconclusive, but the hitch was a sure thing. *If they hitch, they ha'en't!* LHO had 5 rounds of play to work out how to follow smoothly low from king-and-one. This was clearly unethical behavior and lefty got his just desserts when the ace was played from dummy.

Notice that declarer risked the slight odds of a 6-

1 club split in order to give his opponents a chance to employ body English.

The fear of producing a tell has gradually trained most players to make decisions about covering an honor quickly. We have all played the following suit combination:

♣ A1096

♣ KJ85

If West plays low smoothly on the lead of the jack, the ace is played from dummy and clubs are finessed against East. Of course, it is correct to play a high honor first, in case the missing queen is singleton. But the opportunity to elicit a tell improves your chances when you lead toward the high card, as opposed to leading out the ace or king.

The converse of this situation is that occasionally it will be correct to cover, but a good player may feel compelled to play low before he has had the time to work this out. The following hand was played by Andy Robson against a world champion in the West seat, and reported in the New York Times.

```
NONE V.   ♠ 65
DLR: W    ♡ Q95
          ♢ 1054
          ♣ AKJ65

♠ A109832        ♠ J7
♡ K2             ♡ J1064
♢ 6              ♢ KJ982
♣ Q843           ♣ 72

          ♠ KQ4
          ♡ A873
          ♢ AQ73
          ♣ 109
```

West	North	East	South
2♠	Pass	Pass	2NT
Pass	3NT	Pass	Pass
Pass			

The opening lead was the ♠9 (showing 0 or 2 higher) headed by the jack and ducked. Spades were continued, Robson winning the third round. At trick four, the nine of clubs was led from the South hand. This was the remaining matrix:

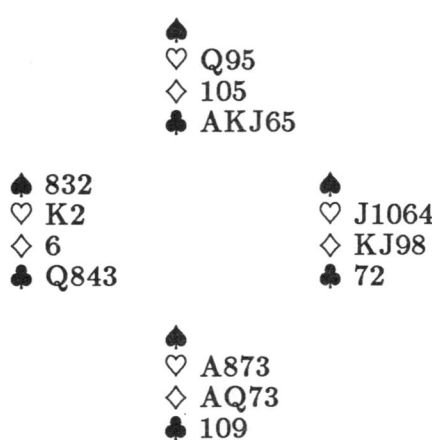

```
              ♠
              ♡ Q95
              ◇ 105
              ♣ AKJ65

♠ 832                      ♠
♡ K2                       ♡ J1064
◇ 6                        ◇ KJ98
♣ Q843                     ♣ 72

              ♠
              ♡ A873
              ◇ AQ73
              ♣ 109
```

At the table, West, the world champion, ducked smoothly. The contract was now certain to be made. Declarer continued clubs, finessing the jack and picking up the suit. The diamond finesse provided the ninth trick. To bring this result about, it was absolutely essential that Robson lead the ♣9 (see Chapter 2), not the ten. However, ducking was a *pure* error by West in that nothing could be gained by playing low. To see this, just switch the seven and ten of clubs. South comes to four club tricks if West ducks by repeating the finesse; should West cover, South can only win three club tricks.

Given ample time, all this could have been worked out, but to the defender in the West chair this *looked* like a situation where a hesitation would be costly.

If you sit down against a very slow player you will have to forego any attempt at reading tempo tells. The same holds for a very fast thinking and playing opponent. Against the rest you will occasionally witness a startling break in tempo midway through the hand. Of course, this means that a problem exists, but the consequences of this are sometimes extraordinary. Weak players will sometimes precipitate a problem by winning quickly and then suddenly becoming aware that all exits look dangerous. You should be attuned to this, not so much because it will picture the hand for you, but because it should alert you to be on guard. With the usual caveat that reading hesitations may be hazardous, consider this hand.

ALL VUL ♠ 84
DLR: N ♡ Q9765
Matchpts ♢ J65
♣ A76

♠ 10965
♡ A10843
♢ A10
♣ K2

North	East	South	West
Pass	Pass	1♡	DBL
4♡	DBL	Pass	Pass
Pass			

In a lighter moment (points that is), you open the South hand with one heart and end up in the stratosphere, in a doubled contract. West begins the assault with the ace and king of spades, East encouraging, and continues with a third round which you ruff with the trump five. At trick four you lead a heart to the ace, but West contributes only the the jack. With nothing extraordinary to look forward to, you ruff your last spade in dummy, West sluffing a small club and exit with a heart to East's king, West again discarding a club. Surprisingly, East goes "into the tank", and his pause also gives you time to think.

One curious think about trances at the table; a fair amount of the time, the player who gets stuck still does the wrong thing. You have yet to know whether this will be the case here, but when East awakes, he puts a small club on the table. What might be going on?

The key question of course is why has East not finished things off by returning a diamond? Undoubtedly from his perspective diamonds were not a safe suit to attack. In other words, East's hesitation has alerted you to the possibility that he holds exactly **one** honor in the diamond suit. Now you see a ray of hope. If East can go wrong once, he may still err a second time. You win the club in hand with the king, lead a heart to the queen on which lefty discards still another club and righty a diamond, and boldly play the jack of diamonds from the dummy. You hold your breath, but sure enough, East covers with the queen. If you are to make the contract you will likely need to find East with a doubleton club, however West's discards give you some hope.

Here is the remaining matrix, as you win the ace, with tentative East-West holdings:

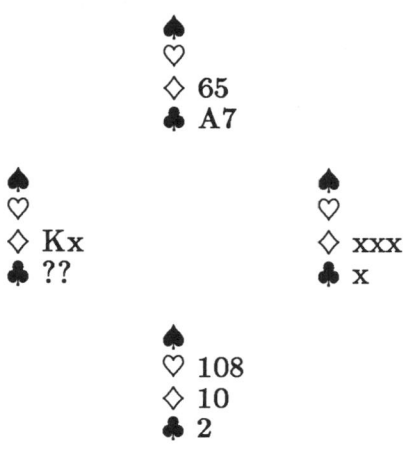

When you cash the remaining two hearts, it gives you great pleasure to note the tension on West's face. Ultimately, he discards his clubs, hoping that partner led low from three clubs to the queen but there is not much hope in his play. Your seven of clubs takes the tenth trick in the end.

These were the complete hands.

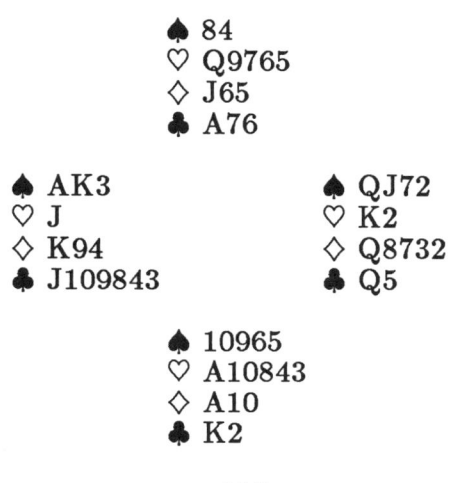

Chapter 9
THERE'S NO A-COUNTING/SIGNAL PLEASURES

It cannot be denied that we all suffer bouts of laziness. At the bridge table this frequently takes the form of failure to count down a hand. There is nothing quite so frustrating as not knowing which card to hang onto at trick 12. How can this failure to pay attention be exacerbated by declarer play? One method, alluded to in the Introduction, is systematically to eliminate high cards, sequentially up the line, in a critical suit, all the while holding a lesser spot. Unfortunately, this is not a reliable technique, only a desperate measure.

As the critical juncture is moved back from trick 12 to trick 9 or 10, counting gets supplemented by inference. Since only a partial count may be available, if the inferences are misleading the counting may be faulty. The most extraordinary examples of this occur when declarer cuts himself off from one or more cashing tricks in dummy. The inference is that he *has* an entry to the board. Sometimes this inference is so overwhelmingly hypnotic that an **exact** count is ignored in favor of the suggestion. Here is a pseudo- guard squeeze from club play:

```
                    ♠ J7532
                    ♡ 632
                    ◇ 92
                    ♣ A107

  ♠ 10                          ♠ AK96
  ♡ AKQJ109                     ♡ 54
  ◇ 1064                        ◇ KQJ3
  ♣ J64                         ♣ K83

                    ♠ Q84
                    ♡ 87
                    ◇ A875
                    ♣ Q952
```

After an unprintable auction, West declared 3*NT*. The opening lead was the fourth-best spade to the king and eight. Notice that Standard carding leads to a confusion here. The eight can be encouragement, indicating the possession of the queen, or it can be count, as some play when failing to cover a card from the board.

Three rounds of diamonds were continued, South winning the third and exiting with a heart. At this point, West cut himself off from the dummy. On the run of the heart suit, the spade "threat" loomed large. This was the situation with five cards remaining:

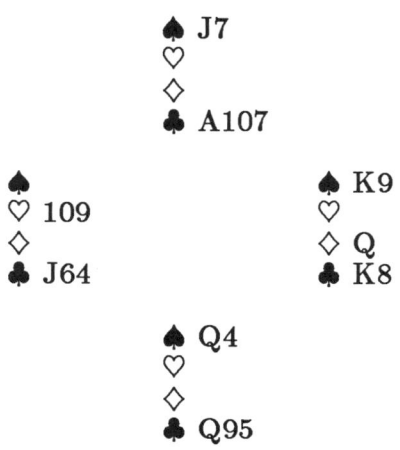

♠ J7
♥
♦
♣ A107

♠
♥ 109
♦
♣ J64

♠ K9
♥
♦ Q
♣ K8

♠ Q4
♥
♦
♣ Q95

As the cards lie, a heart lead, followed by a club toward the dummy, will guarantee 11 tricks for declarer. However, the club cards might as easily have been reversed in the defenders' hands. Instead, West decided to rely on the possibility for error. On the play of the next two hearts, North threw clubs. A club at trick eleven used North as a steppingstone to dummy. This pseudo-squeeze would probably have worked as well against an unwary South hand. To avoid this bridge disaster, the key defensive play must be a spectacular discard of the ♠Q once dummy has bared the club king. To find such a play, South needed to trust his partner's discard of the spade deuce to show a fifth spade. Even so, it takes great courage to ignore the two "winners" remaining in dummy.

Lest this technique be scoffingly consigned to local card-tossing, here is a hand from an invitational international tournament played in the Hague:

117

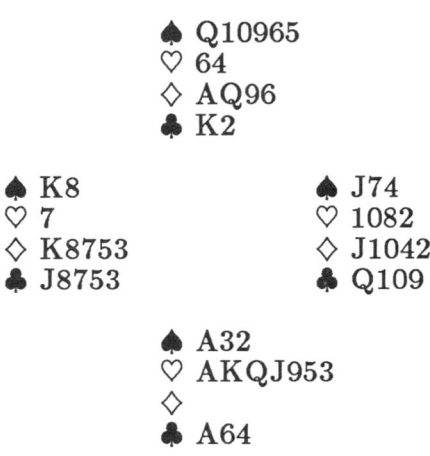

♠ Q10965
♡ 64
◇ AQ96
♣ K2

♠ K8
♡ 7
◇ K8753
♣ J8753

♠ J74
♡ 1082
◇ J1042
♣ Q109

♠ A32
♡ AKQJ953
◇
♣ A64

The bidding in the Netherlands was no more repeatable than that in the local club game. Suffice it to say that Gabriel Chagas, World Team and Pairs champion, landed in 7♡ with the South cards. West found the neutral lead of a club, and Chagas ruffed out clubs and proceeded to run all the hearts. On the play of the last heart, West who was down to a pair of king-eights let go the spade eight and Chagas took the remaining tricks.

What is striking about both these examples is that, in hindsight, the defenses were simply terrible. It would be wrong to dismiss this topic glibly, however. After seeing exactly this sort of disaster occur over and over again, it seems that this type of fraud is actually bound to succeed more than one might expect.

Another place where fear can replace counting is where the opponents are faced with a ruff and sluff. Here are two classics which are still worth repeating:

ALL VUL ♠ 753
DLR: N ♡ AQ32
    ♢ A832
    ♣ 104

           ♠ A4
           ♡ 86
           ♢ J54
           ♣ KQ7653

North	East	South	West
Pass	Pass	1♡	Pass
3♡	Pass	Pass	Pass

The opening lead is the king of spades which you overtake to continue the suit. After winning the queen of spades, partner returns the eight for you to trump, South following. You try the king of clubs, and declarer wins in hand. He plays the ace, king and queen of trumps, West following to all three, and you discard the seven and three of clubs. Now declarer continues with the ten of clubs. When you play the queen, South contributes the jack and your partner follows. Here are the remaining cards:

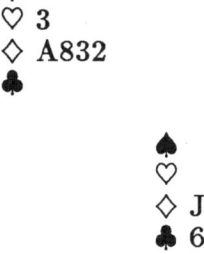

    ♠
    ♡ 3
    ♢ A832
    ♣

        ♠
        ♡
        ♢ J54
        ♣ 65

What do you play? Since you are forewarned, no doubt you have been counting. Declarer's remaining cards are a heart and either three diamonds and a club or four diamonds. In any case, a ruff and sluff will be of no help to South so you continue the clubs. These were the full hands:

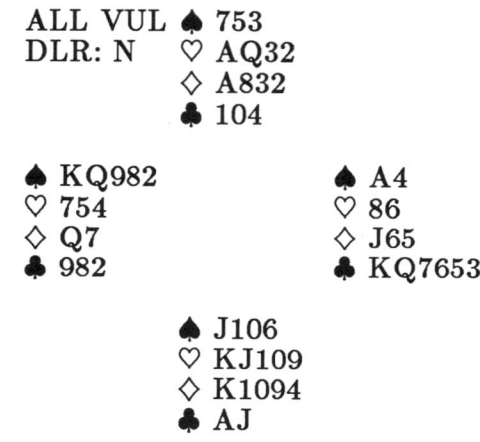

ALL VUL ♠ 753
DLR: N ♡ AQ32
◇ A832
♣ 104

♠ KQ982   ♠ A4
♡ 754   ♡ 86
◇ Q7   ◇ J65
♣ 982   ♣ KQ7653

♠ J106
♡ KJ109
◇ K1094
♣ AJ

Of course, had you switched to diamonds, even deceptively to the jack, South would play for split honors and make his contract.

```
E-W VUL   ♠ Q9532
DLR: S    ♡ 764
Matchpts  ◇ A7
          ♣ 873

♠ A
♡ K10532
◇ 1043
♣ AKJ5
```

South	West	North	East
1♠	DBL	4♠	Pass
Pass	DBL	Pass	Pass
Pass			

Having had a fortified breakfast, you double the final contract and start with two rounds of clubs, East
signaling with the ten initially. The third round of clubs
goes to partner's queen while declarer ruffs with a low
spade.

At this point, South thinks for a bit, then leads the
king of diamonds from his hand, and continues with the
queen to his ace. Next comes the two of trump and you
are in with this matrix facing you:

```
♠ Q953
♡ 764
◇
♣

♠
♡ K10532
◇ 10
♣ 5
```

If partner has the ace of hearts, it looks like 5♣ would have been a laydown. Of course, even with six spades, South's opening would be borderline at best without the ace of hearts. On the other hand, East could easily have the queen of hearts. Unless you lead a heart now, you risk letting South off for down one. The heart seems perfectly safe. After all, even if this runs to a tenace in declarer's hand, you will still get your heart trick – or will you?

Things are not as they seem, for when the heart leaves your hand, declarer rapidly claims.

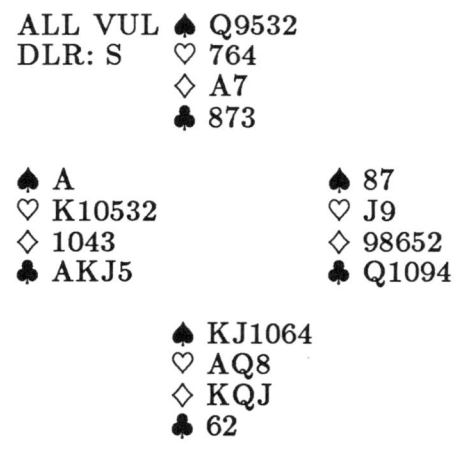

```
ALL VUL  ♠ Q9532
DLR: S   ♡ 764
         ◇ A7
         ♣ 873

♠ A              ♠ 87
♡ K10532         ♡ J9
◇ 1043           ◇ 98652
♣ AKJ5           ♣ Q1094

         ♠ KJ1064
         ♡ AQ8
         ◇ KQJ
         ♣ 62
```

The flip side of not counting out a hand is actually paying attention to the opponents' signals. This allows for a sort of visual parallel to phony cue-bidding and lead-out-of-turn directing doubles (see Chapter 5). While there are undoubtedly good reasons to signal your partner: active defensive hands, continue-don't continue, "your ace is cashing" count showing, and so forth, there are just as many hands where the defense comes to its tricks just by being passive. On hands like those, signals can be made for the benefit of declarer, especially one who puts great stock in them.

One of the greatest feelings of good things to come, I have ever experienced, occurred at a Regional Swiss Teams. The first board had declarer in a small slam and I found a lead into dummy's doubleton ace-king. "Is that attitude, count or suit preference?", he asked, examining my partner's eight spot.

Declarers such as the one above put a high regard on discards, especially if you play a *fancy* method such as upside-down or odd-even, the assumption being that if you've got the tool, you should use it. If you know that partner's contribution to the defense will be inconsequential, you should go out of the way to misdirect. On other occasions, both you and your partner will know where the critical cards lie. Then you can "signal" each other for the cards you don't have. Of course, once you have done this the same opponent will be wary, but one success per match will probably be more than sufficient.

How would you play the following hand:

```
N-S VUL    ♠ Q742
DLR: S     ♡ 105
           ◇ A986
           ♣ K43

           ♠ AKJ93
           ♡ QJ7
           ◇ Q5
           ♣ AQ7
```

South	West	North	East
1♠	Pass	3♠	Pass
4♠	Pass	Pass	Pass

West begins with the ♡A, East contributing the eight. West continues with the king, East following with the two. At trick three a third heart is led. Your call.

This is a famous motif, so you may have seen it before. There is no single answer to this question, but it is definitely advantageous to know your opponents bidding habits. If you like, there have been two messages sent this hand. A positive one: East's peter, or come-on signal, and a negative: West's failure to overcall 2♡ or 3♡ (weak).

Ruffing with the queen will be right whenever East has a trump, but not this time:

```
              ♠ Q742
              ♡ 105
              ♢ A986
              ♣ K43

♠ 10865               ♠
♡ AK963               ♡ 842
♢ J7                  ♢ K10432
♣ 109                 ♣ J8652

              ♠ AKJ93
              ♡ QJ7
              ♢ Q5
              ♣ AQ7
```

Nor would it be right on this similar 4♠ hand:

```
              ♠ Q742
              ♡ 105
              ♢ AK86
              ♣ 743

♠                     ♠ 10965
♡ AK96                ♡ 8432
♢ 109432              ♢ 7
♣ Q962                ♣ KJ85

              ♠ AKJ83
              ♡ QJ7
              ♢ QJ5
              ♣ A10
```

Misdirection can begin as early as trick one. Here is a hand, defended by Edgar Kaplan, and reported in the New York Times. Actually the Times article didn't mention Kaplan's partner, but he certainly figured prominently in the defense.

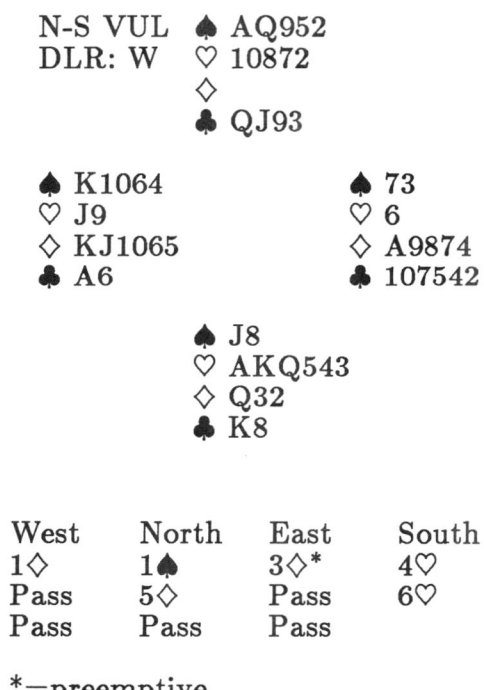

```
N-S VUL    ♠ AQ952
DLR: W     ♡ 10872
           ◇
           ♣ QJ93

♠ K1064              ♠ 73
♡ J9                 ♡ 6
◇ KJ1065             ◇ A9874
♣ A6                 ♣ 107542

           ♠ J8
           ♡ AKQ543
           ◇ Q32
           ♣ K8
```

West	North	East	South
1◇	1♠	3◇*	4♡
Pass	5◇	Pass	6♡
Pass	Pass	Pass	

*=preemptive

There are two ways to play this hand on a non-spade lead. South can try a spade finesse, which works here, or he can try to discard a spade on the third round of clubs. Since South needs to eliminate all his losing diamonds, in practice he cannot afford to pull all the trumps. (If the club ten appears in the first few rounds, then South can revert to pulling trumps and needs to

126

ruff only two diamonds in dummy.)

How do you rate the two attempts? Since West opened the bidding with one diamond, he is more likely to have the king of spades and shortness in the club suit. Certainly, without both diamond honors, South would need the spade king just to make up an opening bid. So it seems reasonable that an expert declarer will rely on the spade finesse. At the table, however, Kaplan, West began with the diamond *king*. When South trumped in dummy, East contributed a **suit preference** nine. The declarer was now absolutely certain that the spade king was with East and West had both diamond honors. He played one round of trump and led a club to the king and ace. After winning West's club return in dummy he continued with the club queen, pitching a spade, and going set when Kaplan produced the heart jack.

Clearly, the diamond nine was a signal made entirely for the benefit of declarer. Nothing possible could have kept declarer from dealing with the spade suit eventually, nor did West need any *help* on the hand.

One way that deceptive signaling can overlap strongly with ideas of masking (see Chapter 2) is when you signal to indicate an honor sequence. Since the declarer will often need to count out the defenders' points, he will often go astray when you find a safe time to signal to show a card which partner, in fact, has.

```
E-W VUL  ♠ A6
DLR: E   ♡ K1074
Matchpts ♢ Q9652
         ♣ 63

♠ Q52              ♠ KJ10873
♡ Q83              ♡ 6
♢ 874              ♢ AK
♣ Q987             ♣ A542

         ♠ 94
         ♡ AJ952
         ♢ J103
         ♣ KJ10
```

East	South	West	North
1♠	2♡	2♠	3♡
3♠	4♡	Pass	Pass
DBL	Pass	Pass	Pass

In the course of a lively auction, South extended himself and was doubled. Still, with East-West able to make some number of spades, the defense needed to find a +300-set. The opening lead was the deuce of spades, and East took the opportunity to drop his king under dummy's ace, thereby announcing a spade honor sequence.

The declarer negotiated the first hurdle successfully,

128

leading a low heart to his hand and finessing West for the queen on the way back. After cashing the king to pull the last trump, he continued with a low diamond from the board. Maintaining the deception, East won honestly with the king. After cashing the jack of spades (thus allowing West the ten-third), East put a low club on the table. At this point, it seemed likely that West began with no diamond or spade honors and only the queen of hearts for his raise. Placing West with the ace of clubs, South followed low to the club and payed up in full to the defense.

Notice that East's play to trick one was reasonably safe. His partnership agreement was to lead high from small spots after giving partner a raise, and to lead low from ten-third and higher. On the other hand, such larceny requires subtle consistency. Had East thoughtlessly played the ace of diamonds to trick five, declarer might have given West the diamond king and guessed correctly in the club suit.

Many authors have discussed false carding intended to confuse attitude signals. It is well known that declarer should use the defenders' methods to *signal* to his left hand opponent to encourage a continuation. For example, against defenders using Standard American attitude signals,

$$\diamondsuit\ 943$$

$$\diamondsuit\ KQ7 \qquad A. \qquad \diamondsuit\ 1085$$

$$\diamondsuit\ AJ62$$

when West starts the king, South should drop the six under East's five. This is really a **mandatory** false card, since playing the two completely gives up. The idea is to convinced LHO that any one of the following holds:

$$\diamondsuit\ 943$$

$$\diamondsuit\ KQ7\ B. \qquad \diamondsuit\ J852$$

$$\diamondsuit\ A106$$

$$\diamondsuit\ 943 \qquad\qquad\qquad \diamondsuit\ 943$$

$$\diamondsuit\ KQ7\ C. \qquad \diamondsuit\ J52 \qquad \diamondsuit\ KQ7\ D. \qquad \diamondsuit\ A52$$

$$\diamondsuit\ A1086 \qquad\qquad\qquad \diamondsuit\ J1086$$

False cards like these are so common that West may be wary and not continue anyway, but he will have more trouble placing your honors.

While interference with attitude signals is a necessary facet of declarer play, it is false-carding to confuse count which is much more allied to error production. Once the defenders begin by attacking in a given suit, there is a natural reluctance for them to stop and switch suits. Partly this is a simple consequence of assets. The defense is generally outgunned from the start, especially in game and slam contracts. Since they frequently find opening leads from some strength, it takes a fair reason to look elsewhere for tricks.

If you are pleased with your opponents' tack, you can sometimes alter appearances just enough to keep things working for you. Recall this hand from Chapter 2:

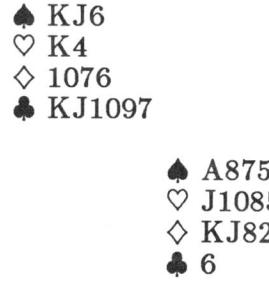

```
              ♠ KJ6
              ♡ K4
              ♢ 1076
              ♣ KJ1097

                        ♠ A875
                        ♡ J1085
                        ♢ KJ82
                        ♣ 6
```

South	North
1NT(13-15)	3NT

When West begins with the heart three, what if South plays the king in dummy and follows with the six from his hand? Now, when East takes the spade king with his ace at trick two, he must decide which of these possibilities is more likely:

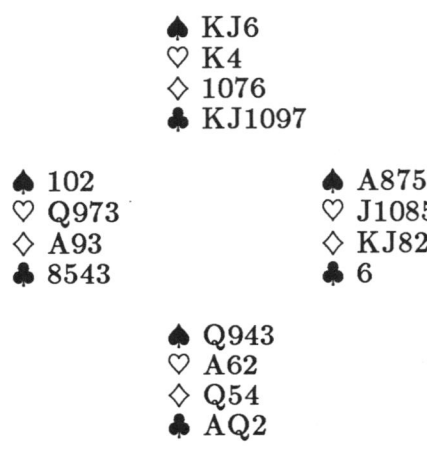

or:

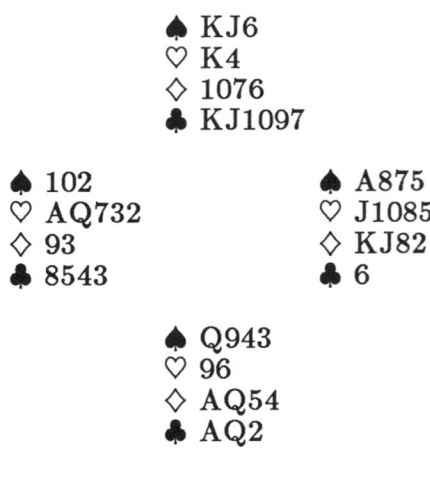

Especially if East gives only a cursory analysis to the defense, he may well just return another heart. If you happen to have the second holding you might wish to play the nine of hearts instead to trick one. If East is the suspicious sort, such a blatant false-card might "wake him up", allowing him to suspect you of the first holding.

It is inevitable that situations will occur in which standard defensive carding leads to ambiguities. Alternative carding schemes may change the nature of these ambiguities, but not the fact that they will happen. It is imperative for a declarer to be sensitive to the possible problems these situations create for defenders. Consider the following three matrices:

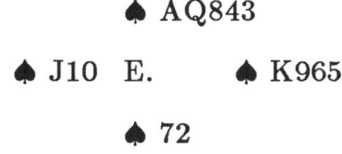

♠ AQ843

♠ J10   E.   ♠ K965

♠ 72

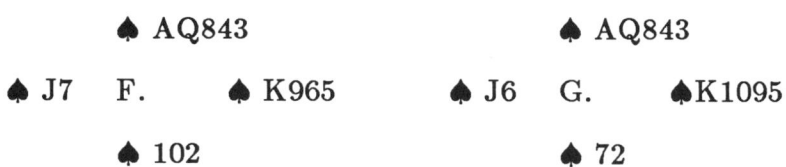

♠ AQ843   ♠ AQ843

♠ J7   F.   ♠ K965   ♠ J6   G.   ♠K1095

♠ 102   ♠ 72

In each of the above, West begins with the standard lead of the jack. This may show either the ten or shortness and typically declarer will be uncertain which.

However, in F, he has a critical advantage over the East defender. Suppose South wins the ace in dummy and continues with the three. East may place his partner with J107 and duck! This kind of pressure play is a close cousin to the cover or don't cover quandaries of Chapter 6.

Once you appreciate the possibilities in matrix F, you will find the extra chance in this hand:

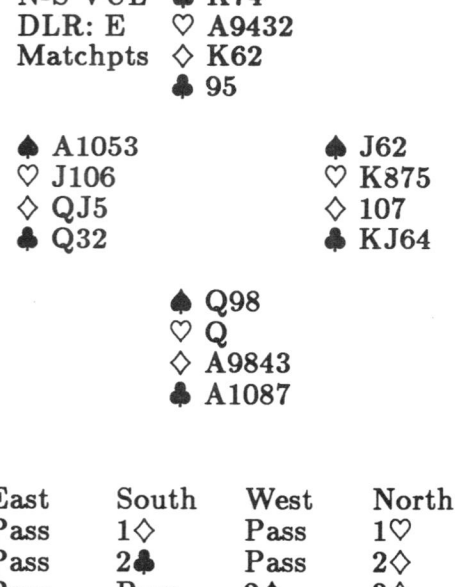

```
N-S VUL   ♠ K74
DLR: E    ♡ A9432
Matchpts  ♢ K62
          ♣ 95

♠ A1053              ♠ J62
♡ J106               ♡ K875
♢ QJ5                ♢ 107
♣ Q32                ♣ KJ64

          ♠ Q98
          ♡ Q
          ♢ A9843
          ♣ A1087
```

East	South	West	North
Pass	1♢	Pass	1♡
Pass	2♣	Pass	2♢
Pass	Pass	2♠	3♢
Pass	Pass	Pass	

After escaping with a very dubious bid, West follows up with the questionable opening lead of the jack of hearts. A natural line of play is to win the ace and duck one round of clubs. Assuming the defense switches to trumps at this point, declarer can win the king, play ace and a club, ruffing in dummy, and return to his hand with a heart ruff to play another club. Whatever West chooses to do at this point, declarer loses just one diamond, one club and two spades, making three.

It would seem that ruffing a heart at trick two is an unnecessary play, but not if East is an imaginative player. He may credit South with an initial holding of the queen-*ten* in hearts or, at least, that possibility. If he plays the king at trick two, declarer will ruff. He can then continue, diamond to the king, heart ruff, spade to the king (West must duck) and the heart nine, which is now high, pitching a spade. Whatever West chooses to do, declarer makes ten tricks.

You sit down, East, in the finals of a Regional pairs event and pick up a not very inspiring collection. Fortunately, (or perhaps unfortunately), sad experience has taught you that paying little attention to bleak hands loses as many IMPs as poorly playing the exciting ones.

Needless to say, the bidding goes on without you.

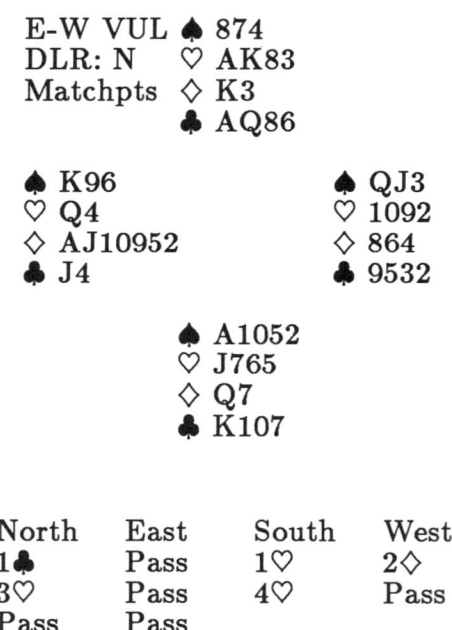

```
E-W VUL  ♠ 874
DLR: N   ♡ AK83
Matchpts ♢ K3
         ♣ AQ86

♠ K96              ♠ QJ3
♡ Q4               ♡ 1092
♢ AJ10952          ♢ 864
♣ J4               ♣ 9532

         ♠ A1052
         ♡ J765
         ♢ Q7
         ♣ K107
```

North	East	South	West
1♣	Pass	1♡	2♢
3♡	Pass	4♡	Pass
Pass	Pass		

The opening lead is the diamond ace, and fearing a spade shift lest declarer hold the king, you encourage. Partner continues with a high diamond which elicits both the king and queen from declarer. At trick three, South leads a trump to the king. Quick! Did you play the nine or ten? If you didn't, then declarer will have no choice but to hope for a doubleton queen of hearts.

Throughout this volume, as throughout bridge, high cards play a crucial role. In Chapter 6, we looked at the errors that follow from the opponents' playing, or failing to play, honors at critical moments. Here we have a related theme in mind, the chaotic consequences that may result from one's own *unnecessary* play of a high card. The first example illustrated a mandatory false card. Here is another:

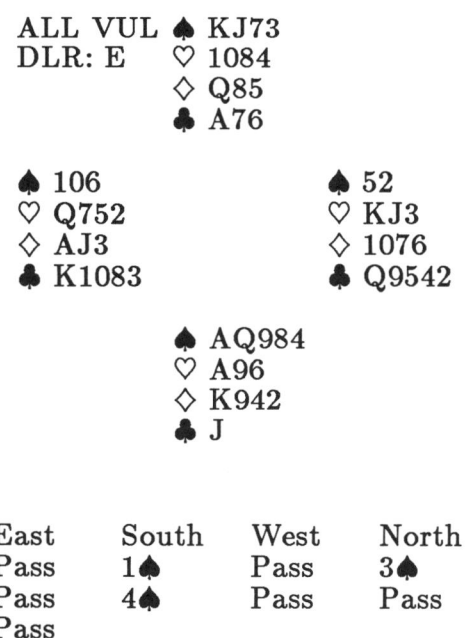

```
ALL VUL  ♠ KJ73
DLR: E   ♡ 1084
         ◇ Q85
         ♣ A76

♠ 106              ♠ 52
♡ Q752             ♡ KJ3
◇ AJ3              ◇ 1076
♣ K1083            ♣ Q9542

         ♠ AQ984
         ♡ A96
         ◇ K942
         ♣ J
```

East	South	West	North
Pass	1♠	Pass	3♠
Pass	4♠	Pass	Pass
Pass			

After a routine auction, West began a heart. Declarer ducked the first round, won the heart continuation, and proceeded to strip his hands of clubs and to pull trump. Finally, he threw West in with his last heart. These were the remaining cards:

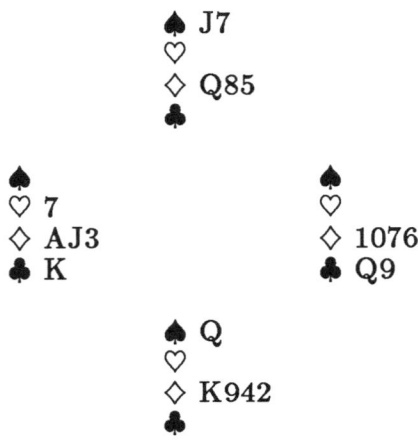

♠ J7
♥
♦ Q85
♣

♠
♥ 7
♦ AJ3
♣ K

♠
♥
♦ 1076
♣ Q9

♠ Q
♥
♦ K942
♣

Needing two more tricks on defense, West continued with the jack of diamonds. South ran this to the king, but when he played the next round of diamonds, lefty played low smoothly and South called for the eight.

It may seem that, as declarer, you have a guess on the previous hand. Indeed, there is no certain play. That was the reason the defender led the jack. But some guesses are better than others. Against a good defender in the West seat, South's play was flawed. He was betting against restricted choice, taking essentially odds of 2:1 against. The reason is the usual one: from a holding containing both the jack and the ten, West might have led either minor honor. From a holding including only the jack- initially just as likely -he would be forced to play that card. Thus, in a good match, with a situation such as this, one should always play

138

for split honors. Obviously this reasoning must be altered against opponents who are inexperienced or when other factors, such as opposition bidding, prevail. Notice, however, that the location of the ace is not relevant to the play of the hand, here. The proper play for South is to cover the diamond jack in dummy. Whether this wins or loses, he should play East for the ten at the next trick.

Even if a declarer is aware of the restricted choice possibilities, he may go against the odds. In the first example, restricted choice actually favors playing East for the queen-ten doubleton. But there are competing inferences. The lead of the diamond ace suggests that West began with six or seven diamonds. With heart length, he might have looked for a side suit ruff, leading from shortness instead. However, suppose declarer needs a good result on the board to try to win. Then he may take a reasonable, anti-percentage line of play, hoping to pick up all the matchpoints.

The first example is interesting for another reason. Switch the queen of hearts and the deuce of clubs and dropping the nine or ten becomes East's only play for two trump tricks.

Now it's your turn. Needing a good result on the last board of a match, you are pleased to pick up a meaty hand. After some healthy optimism and a little competition from the opponents, you find yourself in a reasonable 6♠ contract.

```
        ♠ Q109
        ♡ 6542
        ◇ 632
        ♣ A86

        ♠ A87643
        ♡ AK
        ◇ AKQ5
        ♣ 5
```

South	West	North	East
1♠	3♣	Pass	4♣
4◇	Pass	5♣	Pass
6◇	Pass	6♠	Pass
Pass	Pass		

The opening lead is the king of clubs, and you make a note to congratulate partner on his 5♣ bid. One way to *reduce* the number of errors your side produces is to be honestly complimentary and otherwise SILENT. In the matter at hand, however, it seems that the only problem is how to play the trump suit. Given West's preempt, you might consider playing the queen of spades from dummy, but this is not necessarily wise, since finding East with king-jack-third of spades will force you to rely on a 3-3 diamond split, and if West should have the spade king, you will have more problems, yet. So you

140

play a low spade to the ace and are rewarded by the fall of the jack.

It appears that you are home free, you simply switch to diamonds, intending to ruff the fourth round. Unfortunately, West (Zia when this hand was actually played) produces a nasty surprise for you. He trumps the third round of diamonds with the two. And spades were 2-2 after all.

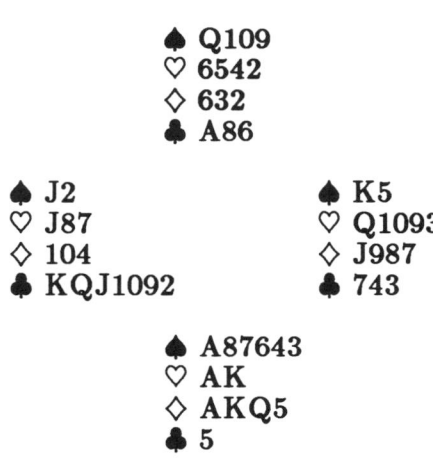

♠ Q109
♡ 6542
◇ 632
♣ A86

♠ J2
♡ J87
◇ 104
♣ KQJ1092

♠ K5
♡ Q1093
◇ J987
♣ 743

♠ A87643
♡ AK
◇ AKQ5
♣ 5

CONCLUSIONS

We have covered a large number of topics in ten chapters, but it is possible to put some perspective on the material. Your opponents at the bridge table make errors strictly in proportion to the opportunities they have to do so. Of course, the ratios are higher for weaker players and lower for stronger ones. But everyone errs. If you can take only one maxim from this book, it is to offer all your opponents frequent chances to go wrong.

While this book has illustrated some particular avenues for errors, occasionally even esoteric ones, the basic issues remain those of pressure and timing. Some errors proceed from the need to act without sufficient information. If that is the case, you must get your opponents to make critical decisions early in the hand. Others proceed from making the opponents believe you have presented them with a useful opportunity, an unexpected chance.

While a bridge book is still current in one's mind, there is a temptation to play the next club game as if all the hands are illustrative examples that just happen to have come too late for inclusion in the text. Well, maybe they will be, but just in case, here is a going-away quiz:

```
ALL VUL  ♠ 98753
DLR: W   ♡ K72
         ♢ AQ2
         ♣ 42
```

```
                    ♠ 2
                    ♡ J5
                    ♢ K10875
                    ♣ J9763
```

West	North	East	South
1♡	Pass	1NT	2♠
Pass	4♠	Pass	Pass
Pass			

After scraping up a meager response, you find yourself defending against a spade game. Partner begins the heart ten, and declarer wins in hand to lead a trump. West wins the spade with the king, and continues ace of trump and a heart. Now South wins in hand, leads a third heart to the dummy and plays ace of diamonds, then queen! What do you do?

Had you not read this book, you would be likely to make the right play. On the other hand, if you have read this book and gone wrong, you may console yourself with the thought that you would probably have figured out how to play the hand. Here is the complete deal:

```
          ♠ 98753
          ♡ K72
          ◇ AQ2
          ♣ 42

♠ AK                    ♠ 2
♡ 109864                ♡ J5
◇ J94                   ◇ K10875
♣ K105                  ♣ J9763

          ♠ QJ1064
          ♡ AQ3
          ◇ 63
          ♣ AQ8
```

Knowing that you needed one king for your bid, declarer realized that the finesses were either both making or both failing. This is an extreme example of Terrence Reese's admonition, "If the finesse is working you don't need to take it." Of course, if your partner had shown up with the king of diamonds, South would not have shunned the second hook.